TEST PREP

Standardized test-taking skills for Reading, Math, and Language Arts

High School

Send all inquiries to:
School Specialty Children's Publishing
8720 Orion Place
Columbus, OH 43240-2111

ISBN 0-7696-3657-8

2 3 4 5 6 7 8 9 10 WAL 09 08 07 06 05 04

Table of Contents

A Message to Parents and Teachers:

- **Standardized tests: the yardstick for your child's future**

    Standardized testing is one of the cornerstones of American education. From its beginning in the early part of this century, standardized testing has gradually become the yardstick by which student performance is judged. For better or worse, your child's future will be determined in great part by how well she or he performs on the standardized tests used by your school district.

- **Even good students can have trouble with testing**

    In general, standardized tests are well-designed and carefully developed to assess students' abilities in a consistent and balanced manner. However, there are many factors that can hinder the performance of an individual student when testing. These might include test anxiety, unfamiliarity with the test's format, or failing to understand the directions.

    In addition, it is rare that students are taught all of the material that appears on a standardized test. This is because the curriculum of most schools does not directly match the content of the standardized test. There will certainly be overlap between what your child learns in school and how he or she is tested, but some materials will probably be unfamiliar.

- *High School Test Prep* **will lend a helping hand**

    It is because of the shortcomings of the standardized testing process that *High School Test Prep* was developed. The lessons in the book were created after a careful analysis of the most popular achievement tests. The items, while different from those on the tests, reflect the types of materials that your child will encounter when testing. Students who use *High School Test Prep* will also become familiar with the format of the most popular achievement tests. This learning experience will reduce anxiety and give your child the opportunity to do his or her best on the next standardized test.

We urge you to review with your child the Message to Students and the feature "How to Use This Book" on pages 6–8. The information on these pages will help your child to use this book and develop important test-taking skills. We are confident that following the recommendations in this book will help your child to earn a test score that accurately reflects his or her true ability.

A Message to Students:

Frequently in school you will be asked to take a standardized achievement test. This test will show how much you know compared to other students in your grade. Your score on a standardized achievement test will help your teachers plan your education. It will also give you and your parents an idea of what your learning strengths and weaknesses are.

This book will help you do your best on a standardized achievement test. It will show you what to expect on the test and will give you a chance to practice important reading and test-taking skills. Here are some suggestions you can follow to make the best use of *High School Test Prep*.

Plan for success
- You'll do your best if you begin studying and do one or two lessons in this book each week. If you only have a little bit of time before a test is given, you can do one or two lessons each day.
- Study a little bit at a time, no more than 30 minutes a day. If you can, choose the same time each day to study in a quiet place.
- Keep a record of your score on each lesson. The charts on pp. 152–155 of this book will help you do this.

On the day of the test...
- Get a good night's sleep the night before the test. Have a light breakfast and lunch to keep from feeling drowsy during the test.
- Use the tips you learned in *High School Test Prep*. The most important tips are to skip difficult items, take the best guess when you're unsure of the answer, and try all the items.
- Don't worry if you are a little nervous when you take an achievement test. This is a natural feeling and may even help you stay alert.

How to Use This Book

1 *Getting Started*

   Read the directions carefully.

   Do the Sample item(s).

   Read the Tip(s).

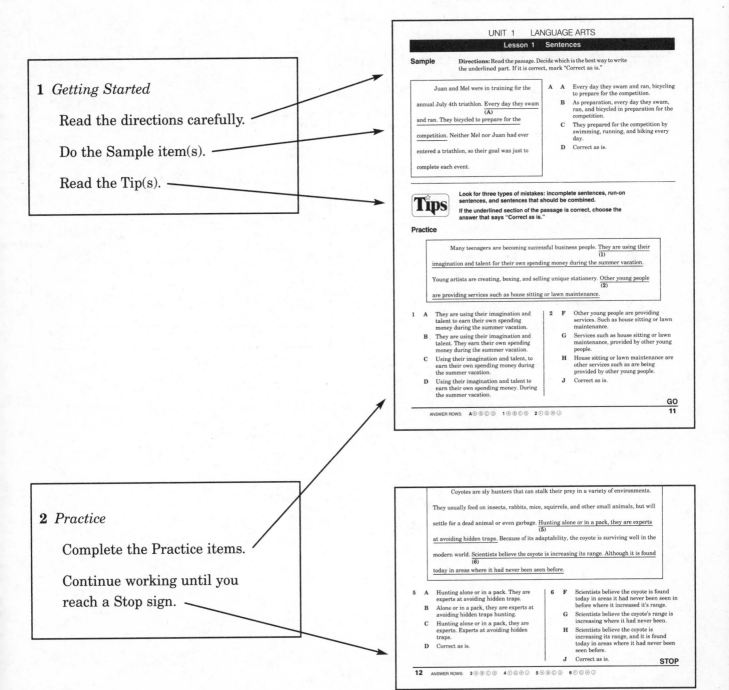

UNIT 1   LANGUAGE ARTS

Lesson 1   Sentences

Sample   **Directions:** Read the passage. Decide which is the best way to write the underlined part. If it is correct, mark "Correct as is."

Juan and Mel were in training for the annual July 4th triathlon. Every day they swam **(A)** and ran. They bicycled to prepare for the competition. Neither Mel nor Juan had ever entered a triathlon, so their goal was just to complete each event.

A   A   Every day they swam and ran, bicycling to prepare for the competition.

   B   As preparation, every day they swam, ran, and bicycled in preparation for the competition.

   C   They prepared for the competition by swimming, running, and biking every day.

   D   Correct as is.

Tips Look for three types of mistakes: incomplete sentences, run-on sentences, and sentences that should be combined.

If the underlined section of the passage is correct, choose the answer that says "Correct as is."

Practice

Many teenagers are becoming successful business people. They are using their **(1)** imagination and talent for their own spending money during the summer vacation.

Young artists are creating, boxing, and selling unique stationery. Other young people **(2)** are providing services such as house sitting or lawn maintenance.

1   A   They are using their imagination and talent to earn their own spending money during the summer vacation.

   B   They are using their imagination and talent. They earn their own spending money during the summer vacation.

   C   Using their imagination and talent, to earn their own spending money during the summer vacation.

   D   Using their imagination and talent to earn their own spending money. During the summer vacation.

2   F   Other young people are providing services. Such as house sitting or lawn maintenance.

   G   Services such as house sitting or lawn maintenance, provided by other young people.

   H   House sitting or lawn maintenance are other services such as are being provided by other young people.

   J   Correct as is.

GO
11

ANSWER ROWS: A Ⓐ Ⓑ Ⓒ Ⓓ   1 Ⓐ Ⓑ Ⓒ Ⓓ   2 Ⓕ Ⓖ Ⓗ Ⓙ

2 *Practice*

   Complete the Practice items.

   Continue working until you reach a Stop sign.

Coyotes are sly hunters that can stalk their prey in a variety of environments. They usually feed on insects, rabbits, mice, squirrels, and other small animals, but will settle for a dead animal or even garbage. Hunting alone or in a pack, they are experts **(5)** at avoiding hidden traps. Because of its adaptability, the coyote is surviving well in the modern world. Scientists believe the coyote is increasing its range. Although it is found **(6)** today in areas where it had never been seen before.

5   A   Hunting alone or in a pack. They are experts at avoiding hidden traps.

   B   Alone or in a pack, they are experts at avoiding hidden traps hunting.

   C   Hunting alone or in a pack, they are experts. Experts at avoiding hidden traps.

   D   Correct as is.

6   F   Scientists believe the coyote is found today in areas it had never been seen in before where it increased it's range.

   G   Scientists believe the coyote's range is increasing where it had never been.

   H   Scientists believe the coyote is increasing its range, and it is found today in areas where it had never been seen before.

   J   Correct as is.

STOP

12   ANSWER ROWS: 3 Ⓐ Ⓑ Ⓒ Ⓓ   4 Ⓕ Ⓖ Ⓗ Ⓙ   5 Ⓐ Ⓑ Ⓒ Ⓓ   6 Ⓕ Ⓖ Ⓗ Ⓙ

3 *Check It Out*

Check your answers by turning to the Answer Key at the back of the book.

Answer Key

Unit 1/Language Arts
Lesson 1 Sentences
Pages 12-13
A. C
1. A
2. J
3. C
4. F
5. D
6. H

Lesson 2 Usage
Pages 14-15
A. B
B. H
1. D
2. H
3. A
4. F
5. C
6. G
7. C
8. F
9. B
10. J

Lesson 3 Writing Mechanics
Pages 16-17
A. C
B. J
1. C
2. F
3. C
4. J
5. C
6. G
7. A
8. H

Lessons 4-8 Writing
(To score your child's writing see the Focused Holistic Scoring Guidelines on page 156)
Lesson 9 Test Yourself
Pages 23-25
A. C
1. B
2. J
3. A
B. J
C. A

4. J
5. B
6. F
7. C
D. H
8. J
9. C
10. G
11. C
(To score your child's writing see the Focused Holistic Scoring Guidelines on page 156)

Unit 2/Reading Comprehension
Lesson 10 Vocabulary
Pages 26-27
A. C
1. D
2. F
3. B
4. J
5. C

Lesson 11 Supporting Ideas
Pages 28-29
A. D
1. B
2. F
3. D
4. H
5. D

Lesson 12 Main Idea
Pages 30-31
A. A
1. C
2. G
3. D
4. H

Lesson 13 Relationships and Outcomes
Pages 32-33
A. C
1. B
2. J
3. A
4. H
5. D
6. G

Lesson 14 Inferences and Generalizations
Pages 34-35
A. B
1. D
2. F
3. B
4. J
5. A

Lesson 15 Evaluation
Pages 36-37
A. D
1. A
2. H
3. B
4. J
5. B

Lesson 16 Test Yourself
Pages 38-41
A. B
1. C
2. F
3. C
4. G
5. D
6. G
7. C
8. H
9. C
10. J
11. A
12. G
13. C
14. J

Unit 3/Mathematics Concepts
Lesson 17 Number Concepts
Pages 43-44
A. B
B. H
1. D
2. H
3. B
4. F
5. C
6. J
7. B
8. F

78

Testing Skills

Language Arts

Sentences:
Identifying sentence fragments and run-ons
Recognizing sentences that should be combined
Recognizing complete sentences

Usage:
Identifying the correct part of speech
Using correct subject-verb agreement with nouns, personal
    pronouns, indefinite pronouns, and compound subjects
Using correct pronoun-antecedent agreement
Recognizing correct verb tense
Using the correct form of adjectives, adverbs, and pronouns
Avoiding double negatives

Writing Mechanics:
Using the fundamentals of spelling
Using appropriate capitalization
Using the fundamentals of punctuation

Descriptive Writing:
Describing an object, person, place, or situation in a written
    composition

Informative Writing:
Describing how to do something in a written composition

Classificatory Writing:
Classifying ideas, objects, or places in a written composition

Comparative Writing:
Discussing opposing courses and supporting one of them in a
    written composition

Reading

Vocabulary:
Using context clues (synonym, antonym, definition and
    explanation, description, or example) to determine
    the meaning of an unfamiliar word or a
    specialized/technical term
Using knowledge of prefixes and suffixes to determine word
    meanings

Supporting Ideas:
Identifying related details
Arranging details/events in sequential order
Following complex directions

Main Idea:
Identifying the stated or paraphrased main idea of a passage
Identifying the implied main idea of a passage
Identifying the best summary of a passage

Relationships and Outcomes:
Identifying cause and effect relationships
Predicting probable future actions and outcomes

Inferences and Generalizations:
Using graphic sources for information
Making inferences and drawing conclusions
Making generalizations
Analyzing information and making judgments
Describing plot, setting, character, and mood

Evaluation:
Recognizing the author's point of view and purpose
Recognizing propaganda and persuasive devices
Distinguishing between fact and nonfact
Comparing points of view

Mathematics

Number Concepts:
Using scientific notation
Using exponential notation
Comparing and ordering rational numbers
Rounding whole numbers and decimals
Determining relationships between and among fractions,
    decimals, and percents

Number Relations:
Using rational number properties and inverse operations
Determining missing elements in patterns
Identifying ordered pairs and solution sets
Applying ratio and proportion
Using exponents and their properties
Evaluating variables and expressions
Solving simple equations
Using number line representations

Geometry:
Identifying lines, rays, angles, and planes
Recognizing properties of two- and three-dimensional figures
Using right-triangle geometry with the Pythagorean theorem
Recognizing similarity, congruence, and symmetry
Recognizing basic geometric constructions

Measurement:
Using metric and customary units
Converting within the metric and customary systems
Finding perimeter, circumference, area, surface area,
     and volume
Recognizing precision

Probability and Statistics:
Using counting methods
Finding probability
Determining the mean, median, and mode
Using frequency distributions

Addition:
Adding rational numbers

Subtraction:
Subtracting rational numbers

Multiplication:
Multiplying rational numbers

Division:
Dividing rational numbers

Estimation:
Estimating solutions

Strategies:
Identifying strategies for solving problems
Determining strategies or solving problems using percentage,
     measurement, or geometry
Analyzing or solving problems using probability and statistics
Making predictions

Problem Solving:
Formulating equations or inequalities
Analyzing or interpreting graphs, charts, tables, maps, or
     diagrams to solve problems

Reasonable Answers:
Evaluating reasonableness

Citizenship

History and Geography:
Understanding historic documents (Northwest Ordinance,
     Declaration of Independence, Constitution, Bill of Rights)
Identifying national symbols
Locating significant places on a map
Reading maps

Law and Government:
Recognizing diversity
Understanding basic economic concepts
Identifying the branches of government and their functions

Recognizing the major economic systems
Understanding federalism
Differentiating among the types of government
Explaining the process of making a law
Understanding basic legal principles
Identifying the functions of political parties
Understanding the role of government officials
Recognizing the importance of voting
Making informed choices
Identifying types of civic involvement

Testing Strategies

Considering every answer choice
Noticing the lettering of answer choices
Working methodically
Indicating that an item has no mistakes
Trying out answer choices
Using context clues
Marking the correct answer as soon as it is found
Prewriting
Focusing on a given topic
Writing with elaboration
Focusing on the steps necessary to complete a task
Writing sequentially
Considering both sides of an issue
Choosing a position
Supporting a position
Discussing opposite positions

Eliminating answer choices
Using key words to locate answers
Referring to a passage to answer questions
Taking the best guess when unsure of the answer
Reasoning from facts and evidence
Skipping difficult items and returning to them later
Using key words, numbers, and figures to answer questions
Finding the answer without computing
Using visual materials to locate information
Computing carefully
Ignoring extraneous information
Indicating the correct answer is not given
Checking answers
Reworking a problem
Rereading difficult questions

Lesson 1: Sentences

Sample   **Directions:** Read the passage. Decide which is the best way to write the underlined part. If it is correct, mark "Correct as is."

Juan and Mel were in training for the annual July 4th triathlon. Every day they swam
                                                                      (A)
and ran. They bicycled to prepare for the competition. Neither Mel nor Juan had ever entered a triathlon, so their goal was just to complete each event.

A A Every day they swam and ran, bicycling to prepare for the competition.

    B As preparation, every day they swam, ran, and bicycled in preparation for the competition.

    C They prepared for the competition by swimming, running, and biking every day.

    D Correct as is.

Look for three types of mistakes: incomplete sentences, run-on sentences, and sentences that should be combined.

If the underlined section of the passage is correct, choose the answer that says "Correct as is."

Practice

Many teenagers are becoming successful business people. They are using their
                                                                        (1)
imagination and talent for their own spending money during the summer vacation.

Young artists are creating, boxing, and selling unique stationery. Other young people
                                                                            (2)
are providing services such as house sitting or lawn maintenance.

---

1 **A** They are using their imagination and talent to earn their own spending money during the summer vacation.

    B They are using their imagination and talent. They earn their own spending money during the summer vacation.

    C Using their imagination and talent, to earn their own spending money during the summer vacation.

    D Using their imagination and talent to earn their own spending money. During the summer vacation.

2 **F** Other young people are providing services. Such as house sitting or lawn maintenance.

    G Services such as house sitting or lawn maintenance, provided by other young people.

    H House sitting or lawn maintenance are other services such as are being provided by other young people.

    J Correct as is.

GO

Lesson 1: Sentences

Have you ever wished you could see to the bottom of the ocean, well, now you
(3)
can. Many resort areas have opened oceanariums—gigantic aquariums that reproduce

the ocean habitat so fish and other sea animals can be observed by visitors. Only a

glass wall separates visitors from fish and marine animals. A viewing area that
(4)
provides a result is a perfect window on the world beneath the sea.

3　**A**　Have you ever wished that now you can see well to the bottom of the ocean?

　　B　Have you ever wished you could see well? Now you can, to the bottom of the ocean?

　　C　Have you ever wished you could see to the bottom of the ocean? Well, now you can.

　　D　Now you can wish to see the bottom of the ocean.

4　**F**　The result is a viewing area that provides a perfect window on the world beneath the sea.

　　G　A viewing area that provides a perfect window on the resulting world beneath the sea.

　　H　The result beneath the sea is a viewing area that provides a window.

　　J　Correct as is.

Coyotes are sly hunters that can stalk their prey in a variety of environments.

They usually feed on insects, rabbits, mice, squirrels, and other small animals, but will

settle for a dead animal or even garbage. Hunting alone or in a pack, they are experts
(5)
at avoiding hidden traps. Because of its adaptability, the coyote is surviving well in the

modern world. Scientists believe the coyote is increasing its range. Although it is found
(6)
today in areas where it had never been seen before.

5　**A**　Hunting alone or in a pack. They are experts at avoiding hidden traps.

　　B　Alone or in a pack, they are experts at avoiding hidden traps hunting.

　　C　Hunting alone or in a pack, they are experts. Experts at avoiding hidden traps.

　　D　Correct as is.

6　**F**　Scientists believe the coyote is found today in areas it had never been seen in before where it increased it's range.

　　G　Scientists believe the coyote's range is increasing where it had never been.

　　H　Scientists believe the coyote is increasing its range, and it is found today in areas where it had never been seen before.

　　J　Correct as is.

STOP

Lesson 2: Usage

Samples   **Directions:** Read the passage. Decide which word or group of words fits best in each space.

It was Judy's first time horseback riding, so the instructor ____**(A)**____ a gentle animal for her. At first, things went well. We walked along a scenic trail until we came to a spot where two streams joined. Then, for some unknown reason, Judy's horse decided to return to the barn. No matter what Judy tried to do, the horse would not be turned. He galloped ____**(B)**____ for the stable through some trees with low branches.

A A choose
    B chose
    C choosed
    D chosen

B F straightly
    G more straight
    H straight
    J straighter

If you are unsure of the answer, try each choice in the blank. Read the sentence with each answer choice to yourself. The correct answer is usually the one that sounds best in the sentence.

Remember, adverbs usually modify verbs, and adjectives usually modify nouns or pronouns.

Practice

You might be ____**(1)**____ to learn that Samuel Morse, the inventor of the telegraph, was also an artist. In fact, when he was a young man, he made his living through portrait painting. Morse hoped to have an opportunity to create the huge paintings that were to decorate the Capitol's walls in Washington, DC. He became discouraged when he was not awarded the commission and turned his energies toward inventing. Today he is ____**(2)**____ recognized as a brilliant inventor and artist.

1 A surprise
    B surprises
    C surprising
    D surprised

2 F wide
    G wider
    H widely
    J widest

GO

Lesson 2: Usage

> The little-known animal called the slow loris is _____(3)_____ named. It is a nocturnal creature that sleeps during the day and creeps along during the night _____(4)_____ for food. The slow loris feeds on insects, birds' eggs, and certain varieties of fruit. It is _____(5)_____ from India to Indonesia and is about the size of a squirrel. Living in trees, the loris spends most of its time inching along branches. It is a member of the primate group and _____(6)_____ resembles a small monkey.

3 A appropriately
   B appropriate
   C more appropriate
   D more appropriately

5 A founded
   B finding
   C found
   D find

4 F searching
   G searches
   H search
   J searched

6 F most close
   G closely
   H close
   J closer

> Without _____(7)_____ , a dozen British soldiers broke into the house. Marsha and her servants were locked in the kitchen, and the Redcoats set up their headquarters in the beautiful mansion. Marsha knew that if they settled in, they might not _____(8)_____ leave and the house would eventually be destroyed.
>
> With the help of her servants, _____(9)_____ managed to climb out a window. She made her way into the barn, where she found and loaded several rifles. She set fire to several bales of hay and began firing the rifles. The confusion was such that the Redcoats _____(10)_____ out of the house, never to return.

7 A warn
   B warned
   C warning
   D warns

9 A her
   B she
   C they
   D their

8 F ever
   G never
   H always
   J usually

10 F flee
   G fly
   H flying
   J fled

STOP

Lesson 3: Writing Mechanics

Samples   **Directions:** Read the passage. Decide which type of mistake is in the underlined part. If it is correct, mark "No error."

Finally, Cal had a day off and the weather was great. He gathered all of his fishing equipment and set off for a relaxing day at the lake. Cal baited <u>his hook cast</u> it into the water,
(A)
and waited patiently. Suddenly, out of the corner of his eye, he caught a movement in the <u>sand. A tiny</u> turtle popped out of the ground
(B)
and began to creep toward the water.

A A Spelling error
    B Capitalization error
    C Punctuation error
    D No error

B F Spelling error
    G Capitalization error
    H Punctuation error
    J No error

For each underlined part, look for one kind of mistake at a time. Look for mistakes in spelling first. Then look for mistakes in capitalization and punctuation.

Practice

Nancy whispered <u>quietly "Just hold still. The</u> ambulance will be here in a
(1)
minute. Everything will be all right."

Her friend, Byron, was lying on the ground holding his eye. He and Nancy had been watching some friends playing war games with paint pellets. The game was usually harmless, and the players wore protective <u>goggls. No one ever</u> dreamed a stray
(2)
pellet might injure one of the spectators.

1 A Spelling error
   B Capitalization error
   C Punctuation error
   D No error

2 F Spelling error
   G Capitalization error
   H Punctuation error
   J No error

GO

Lesson 3: Writing Mechanics

Dear Orlando:
(3)

      Wait until you hear <u>this. Mimi and I are going</u> to be on television next week.
                    (4)

That bone we dug up by the lake wasn't a dead cow after all. It was some kind of

<u>buffalo and the professors</u> at the university came back and looked for more things at
(5)

the spot. I'll tell you all the details next week when you get here.

                                        <u>Your Cousin,</u>
                                        (6)
                                        Paula

3
  A Spelling
  B Capitalization
  C Punctuation
  D No Mistake

4
  F Spelling
  G Capitalization
  H Punctuation
  J No Mistake

5
  A Spelling
  B Capitalization
  C Punctuation
  D No Mistake

6
  F Spelling
  G Capitalization
  H Punctuation
  J No Mistake

      Janet Guthrie became a sports-car racer in 1963. She traveled around the

country racing <u>while she continue</u> her career as an engineer.
            (7)

      Guthrie's dream was to qualify for the Indianapolis 500, and in 1977 she

realized her dream. <u>Unfortunately because</u> of mechanical problems, she couldn't
             (8)

complete the race. The next year she qualified again, and despite a broken wrist,

finished ninth in the race.

7
  A Spelling
  B Capitalization
  C Punctuation
  D No Mistake

8
  F Spelling
  G Capitalization
  H Punctuation
  J No Mistake

STOP

Lesson 4: Descriptive Writing

Almost everyone has had a "mentor," a person they know who has made a difference in their lives. It can be a friend, a family member, someone you have worked with, or somebody else. Describe your mentor in detail and explain how the person has affected your life. Write the description as if it were for a feature in your school newspaper.

Prewriting: Organizing your ideas

Read the directions carefully. Be sure you understand what you are supposed to do.

"Brainstorm" by writing your ideas down on scratch paper. Don't write your composition yet. Just write short notes about a person who has been your mentor. Try to think of all the details you can.

Don't write about things that have nothing to do with the topic. Write about only the person who has been your mentor. Include things such as how you came to know the person, how the person has affected you, and anything else that comes to mind.

Drafting: Writing your composition

Read the notes you wrote for your brainstorm. Decide which ones go together.

Think about the best way to write your composition. You will probably need more than one paragraph, so keep ideas that are related in the same paragraph. Your composition should have a clear beginning, middle, and end.

Think about who will read your composition in the school paper. Write so they will have a good understanding of your mentor. Remember, the person who reads your composition might not know your mentor. Be sure to include all the details you can think of.

Begin writing your composition. Use the notes from your "brainstorm" to write your sentences. Try to express a complete thought in each sentence.

Use adjectives and adverbs to describe your mentor in detail. Use verbs to tell about what the person means to you. If it helps you, talk to yourself quietly about your mentor. Then write down what you are saying to yourself.

Take your time and write carefully. Use the best English you can, but don't worry about mistakes. The most important thing is to write clearly and completely.

STOP

Lesson 5: Informative Writing

Imagine that your school is part of an exchange program involving foreign students. The students have just arrived, and this week they will attend their first high school football game. You have been asked to write a composition explaining what they should do to enjoy the game. You might begin by telling them what to wear. Then continue by explaining other things that will help them enjoy their first American football game.

Prewriting: Organizing your ideas

Read the directions carefully. Be sure you understand what you are supposed to do. If necessary, read the directions twice.

Think about the steps necessary to enjoy a football game. Don't write your composition yet. Just list the steps on scratch paper. Try to remember the routine you follow when you attend a football game. You don't want to leave anything out.

Don't write about things that are not part of enjoying a football game. Tell about finding your seats, player introductions, halftime entertainment, and anything else you can think of.

Drafting: Writing your composition

Read the list you made on scratch paper. Decide which things go together. Are there any other things you should add to your list?

Think about the best way to write your composition. Be sure you write the steps in order, from pre-game activities to leaving the stadium. You will need more than one paragraph, so keep the steps that are related in the same paragraph.

Think about the exchange students who will read your composition. They have never been to an American football game, so write as much as you can so they will be able to enjoy the game. Write about how they should dress, doing a "wave", and anything else that will help them enjoy and understand the game.

Begin writing your composition. Use the steps you listed on scratch paper to write your sentences. Try to express a complete thought in each sentence.

Take your time and write carefully. Use the best English you can, but don't worry about mistakes. The most important thing is to write clearly about what is necessary to enjoy a football game. Don't forget any steps, and put them in the right order.

STOP

Lesson 6: Classification Writing

You have just been chosen to represent your school at a national students convention. The convention will take place during the mid-winter holiday, and it is being held in southern Florida. You will be making the trip alone by airplane. Write a composition for a friend you haven't seen in a long time in which you explain the good and bad things about attending the convention. Explain each of your points completely.

Prewriting: Organizing your ideas

Read the directions carefully. Be sure you understand what you are supposed to do.

Think about going to the students convention. Then think of some good and bad things about the trip. Don't write your composition yet. Use scratch paper to organize your thinking. Try writing a one-sentence "nutshell" that summarizes the good things about the convention. Then write another nutshell about the bad things.

Don't write about anything else, just the good and bad things about going to the convention by yourself during the winter holiday. What would be fun? What would be a problem? How would the other people in your family feel? Will you miss being home for the holidays?

Drafting: Writing your composition

Read your nutshells and the notes you wrote on scratch paper. Decide which ideas go together. Are there any other things you should add to your notes?

Think about the best way to write your composition. You will need more than one paragraph, so keep ideas that are related in the same paragraph.

Think about who will read your composition. Write so your friend will understand the good and bad things about attending the student convention. Remember, you are writing for a friend you haven't seen for a long time. The friend knows a lot about you already but might not be familiar some of the newer things or people in your life. You may have to explain these things or people.

Begin writing your composition. Use your notes to write your sentences. Try to express a complete thought in each sentence.

Take your time and write carefully. Use the best English you can, but don't worry about mistakes. The most important thing is to write clearly so your reader will understand the good and bad things about going to the student convention.

STOP

The young people your age hang out at the local park. Unfortunately, many of them litter the area when they leave. This makes the park unpleasant for other people, and some adults now want young people kept out of the park. Write a letter to the Park Commission explaining your position about this suggestion. Explain your position clearly and convincingly.

Prewriting: Organizing your ideas

Read the directions carefully. Be sure you understand what you are supposed to do. Your letter should state your position regarding the suggestion that young people be kept out of the park.

Think about what would happen if young people were kept out of the park. Is this fair? Where would they go? How would they react? Don't write your letter yet. Use scratch paper to organize your thinking. Just write your thoughts and feelings about being kept out of the park because of the actions of a few young people.

Don't write about anything else except your thoughts and feelings on being kept out of the park. What is your position on this suggestion?

Drafting: Writing your letter

Read the notes you wrote on scratch paper. Decide which ideas go together. Are there any other things you should add to your notes? Keep in mind that your letter will be read by adults on the Park Commission.

Think about the best way to organize your letter. You will need more than one paragraph, so keep ideas that are related in the same paragraph. Your letter should move logically from one idea to another.

Think about the adults on the Park Commission who will read your letter. Write so they will understand your point of view. Your job is to convince them that your position on the issue is sensible. If you do a good job, you may even convince them to agree with your point of view.

Begin writing your letter. Use your notes to write your sentences. Try to express a complete thought in each sentence.

Take your time and write carefully. Use the best English you can, but don't worry about mistakes. The most important thing is to write clearly so your reader will understand your position about keeping young people out of the park.

STOP

Lesson 8: Comparative Writing

Because of budget cuts, your school and another school are being combined. This means that either class size will have to be doubled, or the school will have two sessions. One session will be from 7:00 AM to noon, and the other from noon to 5:00 PM. Write a letter to your local newspaper discussing both solutions. State your position on the issue and give good reasons for your position.

Prewriting: Organizing your ideas

Read the directions carefully. Be sure you understand what you are supposed to do. Your letter should discuss the two options and then state your position on the issue.

Think about the advantages and disadvantages of large classes versus a two-session school day. Which one do you think is best? Don't write your letter yet. Use scratch paper to organize your thinking. Just write your thoughts and feelings about the change.

Don't write about anything else except the two options being proposed to solve the problem and the reasons you favor one of them.

Drafting: Writing your letter

Read the notes you wrote on scratch paper. Decide which ideas go together. Are there any other things you should add to your notes? Keep in mind that your letter will appear in the newspaper and will be read by many different people.

Think about the best way to organize your letter. You will need more than one paragraph, so you should keep ideas that are related in the same paragraph. Your letter should move logically from one idea to another.

Think about who will read your letter. Write so they will understand the options being presented and the one you support. Your job is to convince them that your position on the issue is sensible. If you do a good job, you may even convince them to agree with your point of view.

Begin writing your letter. Use your notes to write your sentences. Try to express a complete thought in each sentence.

Take your time and write carefully. Use the best English you can, but don't worry about mistakes. The most important thing is to write clearly so your reader will understand your position about the proposed solutions.

STOP

Lesson 9: Test Yourself

Sample A

An air show will be held at the

Donleyville Airport this Sunday at 1:00 PM.

The airport's director, Susan Collins, has
(A)

booked a number of quality acts. She has

promised exciting entertainment. Tickets will

be available at the gate.

A **A** Susan Collins, promising exciting entertainment, has booked a number of quality acts as the airport director.

B The airport's director, Susan Collins, has booked a number of quality acts, she has promised exciting entertainment.

C The airport's director, Susan Collins, has booked a number of quality acts and has promised exciting entertainment.

D Correct as is.

The swimming pool is in Peter's town. It has a good safety record for several
(1)

reasons. Swimmers may not run near the pool and must be experienced before they

can use the diving board. Divers may not climb out on the board until the person ahead
(2)

of them is out of the water. Two lifeguards are always stationed in the diving area, and

the "buddy" system is used with young children. The diving area, one of the most
(3)

popular spots in the pool, because of these steps is also one of the safest.

1 A The swimming pool that is in Peter's town, it has a good safety record for several reasons.

B The swimming pool in Peter's town has a good safety record for several reasons.

C In Peter's town, the safety record of the pool is for several reasons.

D Correct as is.

2 F Divers, on the board until the person ahead of them is out of the water.

G Divers ahead of them may not climb out on the board.

H The person ahead of the diver on the board may not climb out of the water.

J Correct as is.

3 A These steps mean that the diving area, one of the most popular spots in the pool, is also one of the safest.

B These steps mean that the diving area is safe. It is one of the most popular spots in the pool.

C The diving area is safe. Because of these steps, it is also one of the most popular spots in the pool.

D Because the diving area is safe, it is one of the most popular spots in the pool because of these steps.

STOP

Lesson 9: Test Yourself

Samples

Yesterday _____(B)_____ the opening of the Family Home next to the medical center. The facility will provide a place to stay for the family members of children who are seriously ill. The Family Home has six bedrooms, a spacious kitchen and dining area, a _____(C)_____ living room, and large indoor and outdoor recreation areas. Several permanent staff members and a group of volunteers will manage the facility.

B   **F**   will mark
     G   marks
     H   mark
     J   marked

C   **A**   comfortable
     B   more comfortable
     C   comfortabler
     D   comfortably

When _____(4)_____ began our hike, we had no idea it was going to turn into a major adventure. We planned to follow the marked trail through the desert, a hike of about five miles. It was not going to be as easy as it sounded.

At mile marker two, I noticed a _____(5)_____ shaped cactus about two hundred yards from the trail. _____(6)_____ nothing of it, Jordan and I walked over and took a few photos. When we finished taking our pictures, we headed back toward the trail. Unfortunately, we never found it.

For the next few hours, we wandered around in the desert. Both of us were becoming frightened. The sun was low in the sky and we knew night would be here soon. Just as we were about to panic, we heard the sound of a vehicle. A park ranger, _____(7)_____ by Jordan's parents, drove into view. To a pair of lost hikers, they were the most welcome sight in the world.

4   **F**   I and Jordan
     G   Me and Jordan
     H   Jordan and me
     J   Jordan and I

6   **F**   Thinking
     G   Thought
     H   Thinks
     J   Having thought

5   **A**   curious
     B   curiously
     C   most curious
     D   more curious

7   **A**   accompany
     B   accompanying
     C   accompanied
     D   accompanies

STOP

Lesson 9: Test Yourself

Sample D

> "What time is it?" asked Jacob. "Wer'e
> <u>   (D)   </u>
> due at the restaurant at 8:00, and I don't want
>
> to be late."

D   **F**   Spelling error
     G   Capitalization error
     H   Punctuation error
     J   No error

> <u>Emily looked at the bicycle</u> and asked, "How do you shift gears? I've never used
> **(8)**
> one like <u>this before?</u>"
>   **(9)**
> "The big shifter moves the chain to a <u>larger sprocket," Answered</u> Kuo, "and the
>   **(10)**
> small shifter moves it to a smaller sprocket. You'll get used to it in no time."
>
> "Everything <u>else makes sense. Lets</u> get going." Emily hopped on the bike and
> began riding away. **(11)**

---

8   **F**   Spelling error
     G   Capitalization error
     H   Punctuation error
     J   No error

9   **A**   Spelling error
     B   Capitalization error
     C   Punctuation error
     D   No error

10   **F**   Spelling error
     G   Capitalization error
     H   Punctuation error
     J   No error

11   **A**   Spelling error
     B   Capitalization error
     C   Punctuation error
     D   No error

STOP

> Your school has a chance to receive a complete video system, including a satellite dish, televisions for each room, and even a mini-studio. The only catch is that every student in the school will be required to watch a 15-minute news show each day, and there will be commercials before and after the news show. Some students want the free video equipment, while others object to being forced to watch news and commercials in school. In a letter to your school board, explain your position on this issue. Be convincing, and explain your position completely.

STOP

Lesson 10: Vocabulary

Sample

Directions: Read the passage and the vocabulary questions. Mark the space for the answer you think is correct.

The Babe

In 1950, Mildred Didrickson was selected by the Associated Press as the outstanding woman athlete of the first half of the century. The "Babe's" athletic accomplishments were legendary, and unlike many other athletes, she <u>distinguished</u> herself in a number of sports.

Born in Port Arthur, Texas, Babe was named to an All-American basketball team while still in high school. At the 1932 Olympic Games, Babe won gold medals in the javelin throw and 80-meter hurdles. Several years later, she became the leading woman golfer in America and captured the title for the Women's U.S. Open three times.

A The word <u>distinguished</u> in this passage means the same as —

A recognized

B high class

C stood out

D noted the differences between

Be careful! The underlined word may have more than one meaning. Choose the answer that gives the meaning of the word as it is used in the passage.

Practice

Is a center like this available in your area?

The new sports medicine and rehabilitation center at the West Hills Hospital has recently been completed. It is a <u>comprehensive</u> facility that will offer a broad range of services, including diagnosis, treatment, and prevention of injuries. Construction of the center took almost a year, but came in under budget. The money saved on construction will be used to buy additional equipment.

The director of the sports medicine center, Sheri Michaels, described it as, "A dream come true. No longer will our patients have to make the two-hour trip to Hoover City for their therapy services. Our new center is equipped to meet all our patients' needs, especially those suffering from sports or occupational injuries. We are particularly proud of our <u>work-hardening</u> program. It will help people injured on the job return quickly and safely. In addition, we will offer a maintenance program to

ensure that their physical condition remains good after their return to work."

Sports coaches at the local high schools are enthusiastic about the new center. All the local schools have established contracts with the center for <u>pre-season</u> conditioning and in-season athletic training. Already, the contracts have paid off. Pre-season injuries among all the student athletes are down more than fifty percent. In addition, because of the pre-season conditioning, athletes are reaching their peak earlier in the season. One coach added that, "Players are enjoying themselves more because they are in better condition and are less likely to be injured."

One of the most popular services offered by the sports medicine center is the conditioning program for recreational athletes. Pre-Ski, for

GO

example, gives skiers a chance to get ready before they hit the slopes. When they make their annual pilgrimage to New Mexico or Colorado, they will be able to ski confidently and not suffer the usual aches and pains that follow the first day on the slopes.

Orthopedic surgeon Sandy Gonzales and athletic trainer Dan Pulaski are starting a special program for senior citizens. The goal of the program is to help the golden-agers become more active physically. "Exercise is one of the best anti-aging treatments we have," commented Dr. Gonzales. "If we can help senior citizens develop the exercise habit, they will live longer and more enjoyable lives."

Many local businesses and organizations have donated equipment to the sports medicine center. The Tyrolean Ski Shop contributed a ski simulator, the First National Bank provided a treadmill, and the Sunset Country Club gave a stationary bicycle. Other businesses have pledged a rowing machine, a stair-stepper, and a whirlpool. The pledges will be fulfilled as soon as the equipment is available from the manufacturer.

One of the unique aspects of the sports medicine and rehabilitation center is its location in the Township Line Mall. This location offers several advantages. It is convenient for patients and staff, has ample parking, and cuts down on both traffic and parking problems at the hospital. Center director Michaels stated that, "We were pleased that the space for our center was available in the mall. In addition to the sports medicine center, we were able to move many of our rehabilitation services out of the hospital to the mall. Our patients love the convenience and the atmosphere, and the hospital administrators were pleased at having so much more room at the hospital for in-patient services such as intensive care, laboratories, nursing stations, and recovery rooms. Our move to the mall will allow the hospital to expand without building an addition. The money we save by not building can be used to upgrade equipment and to improve patient care."

The sports medicine and rehabilitation center is located in the Township Line Mall on the second floor. The telephone number is 555-7328. Hours are from 8:00 AM to 9:00 PM, Monday through Saturday.

1 In this passage, comprehensive means —

A understandable

B medical

C focusing on good health

D including many things

2 The term work-hardening describes an activity that —

F helps people prepare physically for their job

G makes work more difficult and harder to do

H makes a job more secure

J turns an easy job into hard work

3 What does the term pre-season mean?

A Occurring after the season

B Occurring before the season

C Happening now

D Happening later

4 From reading this passage, you learn that a pilgrimage is —

F an exercise program

G the same as skiing

H a religious ceremony

J a journey

5 Pledged means the same as —

A supported

B lent to

C promised to give

D borrowed from

STOP

Lesson 11: Supporting Ideas

Sample

Directions: Read the passage and the questions. Mark the space for the answer you think is correct.

Instant Weight Loss

It was the greatest diet known to humankind, or should I say animalkind! Chipper, my dog, lost at least three pounds in two hours.

Because summer was almost here, it was time for Chipper's annual haircut. The owner of the Pet Emporium spent about half an hour working on Chipper with his electric shears. Not only was his weight reduced, but he looked years younger. Cooler and refreshed, but somewhat confused, Chipper tried in vain to shake his furry coat. Little did he realize it would be returned to him in time for the cold winter weather.

A After Chipper had been sheared at the Pet Emporium, he —

A felt warmer because summer was almost here

B gained a few pounds because his hair was so long

C felt colder because the winter weather was just around the corner

D was surprised when he tried to shake his fur

Skim the passage quickly before answering the questions.

Look for key words in the question. Then look for key words in the passage. The correct answer will often be found near key words in the passage.

Practice

How do you feel about watching other people work?

Nothing is more refreshing on a warm summer day than watching someone else work. And the harder they work, the more refreshing it seems.

Right now, for instance, I'm sitting on my porch and watching young Beth baling the big field on top of the hill. She's been haying that field for over ten years. I know: I put her on the tractor when she was just twelve years old. She was a little shaky at first, but she soon got the hang of it. By the time she was sixteen, she could work that field faster than anyone—even me—without losing more than a few bales.

She picked a great day for baling. It's not too hot, and there's a nice breeze. On Monday, when she cut the field, it was so hot I thought the corn would start popping in the field. Didn't stop her, though. She just stuck that big hat on her head, wrapped a wet handkerchief around her neck, and

set to work. I remember when I would have done the same thing.

While I'm here sipping a lemonade, Beth is driving the "hay train," a tractor pulling a baler and a rickety old wagon. She steers that tractor over the rows of hay like an engineer going down the track, with the wheels of the tractor straddling each row of hay. You'd think someone her size would never be able to see over the tractor, but somehow she manages. When she's finished, her tracks are so straight you'd think she laid them out with a surveying team.

The whole time she's haying, that dog of hers is working just as hard, running along beside her like he's afraid she'll drive away without him. Not much chance of that. Smart as a whip, that dog is, and knows more about herding cattle than most cowboys. Beth sure knew what she was doing when she trained him.

GO

Lesson 11: Supporting Ideas

The way that baler works is sheer poetry. Each row is gobbled up and pushed into shape. When just enough hay is in a bale, the automatic twiner wraps it up and ties it off. A second or so later, the bale comes flying out and into the rickety old wagon. The person who invented that machine sure was some kind of genius.

That's not to say it works perfectly. Every once in a while a bale misses the mark, especially when you are turning the rig at the end of a row. That means, of course, that you have to go back and pick up those bales and toss them into the wagon. In an hour or so, just before sundown, Beth will be doing just that.

I can remember when Beth's mother was her age. She looked an awful lot like Beth does now. Some folks think they still look like sisters. Both of them have hair the color of the summer sun and more freckles than you could count, if you had a mind to. And both of them can ride a horse good as any man. Makes a man proud to see his daughter and granddaughter taking such good care of themselves.

Beth's brother, Frank, is a whole different story. That boy's never done an honest day's work in his life. Says he wants to be a musician, and all he ever does is practice, practice, practice. Must be fairly good at it. He got himself a scholarship to one of those fancy schools in New York. His mother says he's going to be a great violinist. I think he's just going to be a fiddler. Mrs. Stevens, his high school principal, thinks it's wonderful that he's going to New York, but I know she'll miss him come summer and there's no one around to play those concerts in the park. He's some kind of fiddler. But a violinist? I just don't know.

Well, I suppose I should get up and fill this glass again. Not much fun sitting here with an empty glass. I wonder if I could teach that dog to get lemonade for me?

1   Who do you think is telling this story?

   A   Beth's father
   B   Beth's grandfather
   C   Beth's grandmother
   D   Beth's mother

2   Before bales of hay are thrown into the wagon, they must be —

   F   wrapped with twine
   G   dried
   H   turned
   J   untied and separated

3   Which of these people is not mentioned in the story?

   A   Mrs. Stevens
   B   Beth's mother
   C   Frank
   D   John

4   In this story, the way Beth drives the tractor is compared to —

   F   a hay train
   G   poetry
   H   an engineer driving a train
   J   a pilot flying a plane

5   At some time in the past, the person telling this story —

   A   owned the tractor, baler, and wagon that Beth is using now
   B   bought the dog that Beth trained
   C   played the fiddle and taught Frank how to play
   D   hayed the field like Beth is doing now

STOP

Lesson 12: Main Ideas

Sample

Directions: Read the passage and the questions. Mark the space for the answer you think is correct.

Summer Studying

Larry wanted to improve his scores on the achievement tests he would be taking in the fall. He bought a book that would help him, and promised himself that he would spend an hour a day during the summer studying it.

The promise was hard to keep. He was busy working part-time, playing summer sports, helping out at home, and spending time with his friends. He was determined, however, and kept his promise, even if it meant working very late at night or early in the morning. Happily, his hard work paid off, and when Larry took his test, his score was among the highest in the class.

A The main idea of this story is that —

A studying during the summer is hard, but it is usually worth it

B the best way to improve test scores is to study during the summer

C school is just as important as friends, family, and sports

D an hour a day of summer study will probably raise your test scores

The main idea should describe the content of the whole passage. Be careful not to choose an answer that is a detail from the passage.

Practice

A Surprising Health Problem

Do you handle stress by clenching or grinding your teeth? If you do, you may be in for an unpleasant surprise. Many people know that grinding their teeth may cause them to chip or break, but few realize that headaches, dizziness, nausea, and even backaches may be the result of this habit.

Research has revealed that grinding your teeth may damage the joints on either side of your jaw. This causes the jaw to move out of its normal position and strain the muscles holding the head in place. This tension on the neck causes spasms and other complications. And if your jaw is stiff when you wake up, you may have been grinding your teeth in your sleep.

There are dental procedures available that will solve the problem. If you think you may be a nighttime tooth grinder, or if you clench your jaw when under stress, see your dentist.

1 Which of these is the best summary of the passage?

A A dentist is the best health professional to see if you grind your teeth or clench your jaw.

B The muscles in your jaw can be injured if you grind your teeth.

C Grinding your teeth or clenching your jaw can cause a variety of health problems.

D Some people grind their teeth at night without knowing it and should see a dentist.

GO

Lesson 12: Main Idea

The First Americans

There was a time long ago when a land bridge connected Asia and North America. The first settlers in North America crossed this land bridge from what is now Siberia to Alaska. The people who made this initial crossing were probably following the animals they used for food. Some people believe the animals might have been mammoths, extinct creatures that are relatives of today's elephant.

Eventually, the oceans rose and the land bridge between the continents disappeared. The settlers, who I shall call the "First Americans," could not return to their homeland. They would have to survive in the New World they had discovered.

For the next few thousand years, the First Americans migrated south and east throughout North and South America. They made the journey all the way from Alaska to the southern tip of South America, a distance of more than 10,000 miles. Along the way, they established many different civilizations.

In the far north, above the Arctic Circle, the First Americans became hunters of the ocean. They built boats of animal skins and hunted or fished for their food. In the brief summer, they gathered berries and other plants. In the winter, they stayed in lodges much of the time preparing for the next summer. It was a hard life, but they learned to survive in these harsh conditions.

Farther south, in what is now Arizona, Utah, Colorado, and New Mexico, the First Americans became cliff dwellers. They began by living in caves that already existed in the cliffs. They discovered how to add to the caves by building structures of wood and stone. The dwellings they constructed in many ways resembled today's apartment buildings.

The First Americans of the Southwest learned to irrigate the desert. They built a system of dams and canals so they could store and use water almost any time of year. They were so successful they could raise fruits and vegetables that were not found naturally in the desert.

In Mexico and South America, the First Americans founded civilizations that were among the greatest in the world. They built huge pyramids, lived in fabulous cities, and made great advances in science and mathematics long before the Europeans arrived. They also discovered foods like corn and potatoes that became important sources of nutrition for the rest of the world.

2   What is the best summary of this passage?

F   People in North and South America established a variety of cultures.

G   People from Asia crossed a land bridge and settled North and South America, establishing many different cultures.

H   The land bridge that once connected North and South America has now disappeared, but it allowed the settlement of the New World.

J   European settlers did not realize that the New World had many rich cultures.

3   If you had to choose another title for this passage, which of these would be best?

A   Trapped in the New World

B   The Cultures of the New World

C   Wanderers from Asia and Their Cultures

D   The Earliest Settlers in the New World

4   Implied in this story is the idea that —

F   the original settlers of the New World had little to offer European explorers

G   European explorers were surprised to find so many rich and different cultures in the new world

H   Europeans were not the first to discover or establish advanced civilizations in the New World

J   elephants traveled from the New World to India and Asia

STOP

Sample

Directions: Read the passage and the questions. Mark the space for the answer you think is correct.

Preparing for a Vacation

Before leaving on vacation, arrange to have your mail and newspapers picked up. Set timers on lights and radios so they will come on at specific times each day. A home that is dark and quiet all day and night is an open invitation.

It is also helpful to move valuables away from windows where they might be seen from the street. Criminals often choose houses where there are a number of valuable objects in clear view.

Finally, let your neighbors know where you will be and when you are expected to return. If possible, leave an emergency phone number with them. If a problem ever arises, they will be able to reach you at once.

A Why would burglars be more likely to break into a house where valuables are visible through a window?

A It will be easier to remove them through the window.

B Burglars prefer working where the light is good.

C They will be certain that they will find objects worth stealing.

D They will have an easier time selling valuables if they see them first.

Skim the passage, then read the question and the answer choices carefully. Reread the part of the passage that will help you choose the right answer.

Take your best guess if you are unsure of the answer.

Practice

How do you think this camping trip affected the writer?

Monday: Here I am, in the middle of nowhere. This camping trip idea is not getting off to a very good start. It's raining, the tent leaks, and we're ten miles from the nearest electricity and running water. The hike in seemed to take forever, and I still can't understand how it could all have been up hill! How did I ever let my brother talk me into this? When we get home—if we ever get home—he's going to have to do something fabulous to get back on my good side. Maybe he should sponsor a shopping spree at the mall!

Tuesday: Things are looking up. The sun came out today, so we were able to leave the tents and dry out. We're camped at the edge of a small lake that I couldn't see before because of the rain and fog. The mountains are all around us, and the forest is absolutely beautiful. We spent most of the day dragging everything out of our backpacks or tents and putting it where the sun could dry it out. After lunch we headed down to the lake for a swim. Later in the afternoon we tried to catch fish for dinner, but the fish were smarter than we were. At night, we built a fire, and my brother and his friend sang songs I never heard of; I'm not sure anyone ever heard of them. It definitely wasn't MTV, but it was kind of fun.

Wednesday: We hiked to the far side of the lake and climbed to the top of a small peak. From there we could see how high the other mountains were and how far the forest spread around us. On the way up we passed through a snowfield! Here it was, the middle of July, and there was still snow on the ground. One of Art's friends explained that the snowfield would last another few weeks before it melted. He said the snow on the higher mountains stayed there year-round. He called them glaciers,

GO

Lesson 13: Relationships and Outcomes

which surprised me. I thought glaciers were only found in places like Alaska or the South Pole.

Thursday: I caught my first fish! Some of the group went to look for fossils and the rest of us followed the stream that fed the lake. After about two miles, we came to a section that Carol said looked "fishy." She had a pack rod, which comes apart into sections that can be carried in a backpack. She let me cast it, and I caught a fish on my first try. It was a cutthroat trout about 12 inches long. It got this name because it has red slashes under its gills. I put it back in the water. It was just too pretty to eat for lunch. I caught a few more and so did Carol, but they were all returned to the stream. We enjoyed freeze-dried macaroni and cheese for lunch. It actually tasted pretty good, although we were so hungry even liver would have tasted okay.

Friday: I can't believe we are going home already. It will be nice to get a hot shower, sleep in a real bed, and eat junk food, but the trip has been wonderful. We're already talking about another camping adventure next year where we canoe down a river in Maine. It's hard to believe, but I think this city girl has a little country blood in her veins.

1 The writer of this journal ended up on the camping trip because —

A she enjoys camping
B her brother influenced her
C her sister influenced her
D she wanted to be with her friends

2 Why do you think the writer's friend, Carol, had a pack rod with her?

F She could not afford to buy a regular fishing rod.
G She needed it because fish was their main source of food.
H The writer of the journal asked her to bring it.
J She expected to go fishing while they were hiking.

3 In this journal, you learn that snow and glaciers are found in some mountains in the summer. This is possible because —

A the higher you go, the cooler the temperature becomes
B the higher you go, the warmer the temperature becomes
C the stone in the mountains keeps the ground cool
D wind rarely blows in the mountains

4 In the future, it is likely that the writer of this journal will —

F eat fish she catches, even if they are pretty
G try to convince her brother not to go on camping trips
H be more eager to go on camping trips
J be less eager to go on camping trips

5 Why was there no electricity at the place they set up camp?

A The campers brought batteries so they could use electric appliances.
B Electricity shouldn't be used near streams or lakes.
C The storm blew the power lines down.
D It was too far from the main power line.

6 When the writer of this journal returns to school, she will probably —

F tell her friends what a miserable time she had camping
G tell her friends what a good time she had camping
H convince her friends that they should come shopping with her at the mall
J eat freeze-dried food rather than regular food

STOP

Lesson 14: Inferences and Generalizations

Sample   **Directions:** Read the passage and the questions. Mark the space for the answer you think is correct.

More Than Just a Barn

On the outskirts of London, England, there is a barn that would be a major tourist attraction in America. The barn is built from the remains of a ship and dates back to the eighteenth century. What makes this barn special is that historians know which ship provided the materials for it. While examining the barn, researchers also investigated the farmhouse nearby. The door of the farmhouse was made from the same wood as the barn and was decorated with small, carved, English flowers. If you have not guessed by now, the ship was the *Mayflower*, which brought the Pilgrims from England to America.

A Why do you think the barn is not a tourist attraction in England?

A There are many other tourist attractions in England.

B The Pilgrims are less important to the British than they are to Americans.

C Not many people in England know who the Pilgrims were.

D There are many old barns in England made from famous ships.

The correct answer may not be stated directly in the passage. You may have to "read between the lines." This will help you understand what the writer means and choose the correct answer.

If a question is too hard, skip it and come back to it later.

Practice

Our Solar System

The earth is part of an astronomical grouping called a solar system. At the center of the solar system is a star, which in our case is called the sun. Surrounding the sun and revolving around it are planets and other bodies. Our solar system has nine known planets, some of which have moons of their own. In addition to planets, there are smaller bodies revolving around the sun. These are called asteroids, and some people believe they are fragments of one or more planets that broke apart for an unknown reason.

Pluto is the smallest planet. It is also the farthest from the sun. Discovered in 1930, Pluto was predicted by mathematical calculations before it was actually found. Its orbit around the sun is so unusual that it can temporarily be closer to the sun than Neptune, its nearest neighbor.

The largest planet is Jupiter, with a diameter more than ten times that of the earth. It

is a mysterious planet, made up chiefly of methane and ammonia, with some hydrogen and helium present. On earth, these substances are gases, but Jupiter is so cold that they can exist as solids and liquids. The frozen gases surround a rocky core that scientists believe is about the same size as the earth.

The most spectacular planet is Saturn, which is surrounded by a series of rings. At some times, these rings can be seen in the evening sky with just a low-power telescope or even binoculars. No one is quite sure what the rings are made of, but data from the space probes Voyager I and II are being analyzed by scientists in the hope of finding an answer.

Mars and Venus are the planets that are nearest the earth. Because they are so close, people in the past wondered if they might be inhabited. Scientists know this is not possible, but there is a

GO

Lesson 14: Inferences and Generalizations

slight chance that some form of life might exist on one or more of the planets. Both Mars and Venus have atmospheres, and their temperature range is much closer to earth's than other planets'. Even if a life form is discovered on either planet, you can be sure it will be very different from the space creatures described in science fiction.

The planet that is nearest the sun is Mercury. It is about 36 million miles from the sun, which is equal to .4 Astronomical Units.* Mercury rotates on its axis every 59 earth days, but its year is only 88 earth days. Because of its slow rotation and nearness to the sun, the surface of Mercury facing the sun is very hot, perhaps as hot as 800° Fahrenheit. The side away from the sun is much cooler, perhaps as cold as -300° F.

The earth is unique in the solar system because it can support life. The temperature range is just right, it has an atmosphere of life-supporting gases, and it is blessed with an abundance of free water. If any of these ingredients had been missing, our planet would be just as lifeless as its neighbors.

* An Astronomical Unit or A.U. is equal to the average distance between the earth and the sun. This is approximately 9.30×10^7 miles or 1.50×10^8 kilometers.

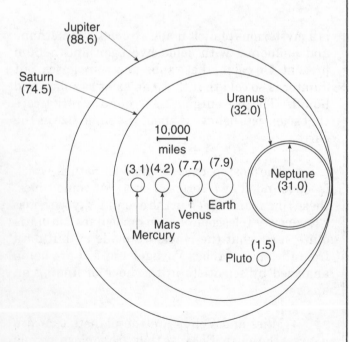

The diameters of the planets are shown in parentheses. The numbers in parentheses represent thousands of miles.

1 In what circumstances would you be most likely to measure things using Astronomical Units?

A When one of the objects was the sun

B When the objects were very large

C When the objects were near the earth

D When the distances between the objects were very great

2 Look at the chart on the left. What is the diameter of Venus?

F 7700 miles

G 77,000 miles

H 7.7 A.U.

J 7.7 times the diameter of the earth

3 Which two planets are closest in size?

A Venus and Mars

B Neptune and Uranus

C Jupiter and Saturn

D Pluto and Neptune

4 Which of these is the best definition of the term year?

F 365 days

G One Astronomical Unit

H The time it takes a planet to rotate on its axis

J The time it takes a planet to revolve around the sun

5 The average temperature on earth is —

A warmer than on Jupiter

B colder than on Jupiter

C about the same as Pluto

D warmer than Mercury

STOP

Lesson 15: Evaluation

Sample

Directions: Read the passage and the questions. Mark the space for the answer you think is correct.

This is a "Letter to the Editor"

Dear Editor:

   Able-bodied people who park in spaces for the handicapped are both thoughtless and unfair. They don't realize how difficult it can be for a person with a disability to find a place to park and leave the car safely. The inconsiderate people who take these special places often say, "It's only for a minute." It's not just for a minute, it's for as long as it is convenient for them. And while they shop or run errands, someone who truly needs the parking spot is struggling to find one.

Eve Lang

A Why did Eve Lang write this letter to the editor?

   A The letter might cause more towns to set aside parking for the disabled.

   B It might encourage people to make laws about parking in spaces for the disabled.

   C So disabled people will know that there are special parking spaces for them.

   D Some people might feel so ashamed that they will avoid parking in spaces set aside for disabled people.

Use the information in the passage to choose the answer you think is correct. If an answer choice has nothing to do with the passage, then it is wrong and can be eliminated.

Take your best guess if you are unsure of the answer.

Practice

An Unhappy Traveler

Phyllis recently took a vacation with her family. Their airplane flights were awful, so Phyllis decided to write a letter of complaint to the airline.

To whom it may concern:

   This letter describes the worst travel experience I have ever had. The problems we had were the result of poor management and thoughtless employees. Your airline should be ashamed of treating its customers so poorly.

   On January 5, we arrived in Denver from Houston and checked in for our next flight. It wasn't long before the agent announced that our flight would be delayed because of a mechanical problem. The equipment was in Aspen, and they expected it to be repaired soon.

   Soon shortly turned to much later, and during the delay, weather temporarily closed the Aspen airport. The weather cleared in Aspen and the plane took off very late for Denver. While it was in the air, the agent announced that the plane would be used for the next flight and that our flight was being cancelled.

   This cancellation struck me as being unfair. There was a mad scramble as the 50 or so passengers scheduled for our flight fought for seats on later flights. When the dust settled, we were wait-listed on the 9:00 flight the next morning. We had to spend the night in the airport.

   Coming home was no better. Because of a mechanical problem, it looked like we would miss our connection in Denver. The agent assured us they would hold the Newark flight for us. Needless to say, the flight to Houston taxied out as we pulled

GO

into the gate. Arrangements were made for us to take the next flight, so we sat in the airport for five hours. When we finally arrived in Houston, our skis were missing. As of this writing, the skis have not been found.

Nothing you can do will make us feel better about our flights. If you are a responsible business, however, you will do what you can to see that passengers in the future are treated better.

With great displeasure,
Phyllis Dooley

This is the response Phyllis received.

Dear Ms. Dooley:

Please accept our apology for your recent inconvenience. Situations beyond our control often occur in airline travel, and unfortunately, passengers often suffer because of them.

The problem you experienced was based on a business decision. By cancelling your flight, we were able to maintain our schedule for all the remaining flights. No passengers, other than the ones on your flight, were inconvenienced. In other words, more than 500 people arrived at their destinations on time, while only 50 were late.

We checked with the supervisor on duty when your problem occurred. He informed us that several of the staff involved were new employees and were unfamiliar with our procedure for assigning seats after a cancellation. Because you checked in early, you should have been assigned seats on the next available flight ahead of many other travelers. The "mad scramble" you describe should never have happened.

Our corporate policy is that if travelers are dissatisfied, we will give them a free ticket anywhere we fly. We want to keep you and your family as customers, and we hope you will accept the enclosed tickets. We also hope that your complimentary flight is an enjoyable one.

Sincerely,
Marcia Green
Customer Relations

1 When Phyllis wrote her letter, she felt —

A annoyed

B tired

C satisfied

D responsible

2 Which of these is an OPINION?

F Weather closed the Aspen airport.

G The skis were still missing.

H There was a mad scramble for seats.

J Phyllis's family sat in the airport for five hours.

3 The purpose of the first paragraph of Marcia Green's letter is to —

A make Phyllis feel angry

B suggest the problem was not their fault

C make Phyllis feel good

D accept complete blame for the problem

4 The second paragraph of Marcia Green's letter says, in effect, that —

F the airline wanted to do the fair thing for all the passengers

G cancelling the flight was an accident

H weather was the reason for the cancellation

J the airline had a good reason for cancelling the flight

5 Phyllis Dooley and Marcia Green —

A disagree on most points

B agree that a problem occurred

C blame the weather, not the airline

D were not affected personally by the incident

STOP

Lesson 16: Test Yourself

Sample

When Blood Won't Clot

Hemophilia is a hereditary disease that interferes with the blood's ability to form clots. Men who have the disease are in constant danger of bleeding to death from even minor injuries.

The disease is passed down from generation to generation, but it affects only males. Except in rare cases, females are the carriers but are not affected by the symptoms of the disease. In a family where the father is normal and the mother is a carrier, chances are that one out of two sons will suffer from hemophilia.

A Which of these groups is most likely to have hemophilia?

A Girls with a mother who is a carrier

B Boys with a mother who is a carrier

C Husbands whose wife is a carrier

D Wives whose husband is a carrier

Ski Area Debate

The Rendezvous Peak Ski Area has received final approval from the federal government to lease more than 20,000 acres of national forest land. The only hurdle that stands between the developers and their dream is next week's town <u>referendum</u>. The vote, which will take place on Tuesday, will determine the fate of the project. Editorials on this and the next page summarize the positions held by those opposing and supporting the Rendezvous Peak Ski Area. We urge all our subscribers to read the editorials and think carefully before making their decision in the voting booth on Tuesday.

Everybody benefits from Rendezvous Peak.

The opening of Rendezvous Peak will be a turning point for our region. It will reverse our economic downturn by providing more than a thousand jobs and bringing in hundreds of thousands of visitors a year. We desperately need this vitalizing influence.

Opponents of the ski area argue that it will hurt the environment. Phoebe Blanchard, a consultant from Environmental Designs, points out that the ski area will actually improve the environment. Rendezvous Peak is now a "lodgepole pine desert," she comments. "The dense pine forest that covers the mountain supports very few animal species and is in danger of falling victim to plant diseases. When the runs are cut for the ski area, shrubs, grasses, wildflowers, and new tree species will quickly move in. A variety of animals will thrive in this new environment, including deer, elk, bear, and small mammals. The number of song birds will increase almost at once, and the ponds used to supply artificial snowmaking equipment will attract waterfowl. In addition, the runs will act as firebreaks if a forest fire ever occurs." Blanchard's consulting firm was hired by the National Forest Service to develop an environmental impact plan.

In addition to the jobs the ski area will provide, it will become a source of tax revenue. After the area has been created, it will pay more than $2,000,000 a year in taxes. This will allow us to build the new school we need, renovate our parks and streets, and complete the low income housing project that senior citizens have been requesting. The state has promised to improve the highway if the ski area is approved. Moreover, if the ski area attracts the number of tourists that is projected, the legislature has pledged funds to improve the airport. Universal Airlines has indicated it will begin service from both coasts and from Chicago.

Everybody benefits from Rendezvous Peak. Property values will increase, store owners will see their business soar, and young people will no longer have to move away to find work. The environment will be improved, and all of us will have a recreation area to enjoy. I urge you to vote yes on Tuesday.

Cindy Koster
Marshall County Chamber of Commerce

GO

Lesson 16: Test Yourself

Who needs Rendezvous Peak?

Rendezvous Peak is a natural gem that should remain untouched. It is the most accessible wilderness area in the state and offers an incomparable variety of recreation opportunities. Developing the area into a ski resort will turn it into a playground for yuppies and will make it more difficult for hikers, hunters, and fishermen to use the mountain.

The lodgepole pine forest that covers the mountain is a natural wonder. It contains old-growth trees that will not be replaced for hundreds of years if they are cut down. The ski runs planned for the mountain will be scars that won't heal. Sure, they may serve as firebreaks, but how many forest fires do we have? The last major fire was in 1943, and only about 1,000 acres were affected. Besides, forest fires are nature's way of revitalizing forests. Ski runs are not.

Cutting ski runs will also remove about 5,000 acres of "oxygen engines." The mature trees cut to accommodate skiers currently remove thousands of tons of carbon dioxide a year and replace it with oxygen. This "environmentally safe" ski area will be hastening global warming.

The jobs promised by the developers will be seasonal. When spring arrives, most of the workers will be on their own until the next ski season. There is also no guarantee that local people will get the jobs. It is likely that many outsiders will come to our area seeking work as soon as jobs become available. Who's to know if these job seekers are the kind of people we want in our town?

The financial benefits to the town will be far outweighed by the costs. Most of the tax revenue generated will have to be spent on maintaining roads damaged by heavy traffic, increased police patrols, highway signs, and the like. Very few tax dollars will ever reach the citizens of town, and it is highly unlikely they will be put toward the building of a new school. And as for the new highway and larger airport, who needs them? Our town is a quiet retreat from the hustle and bustle of the world outside. A larger airport and wider highway will turn us into an upscale neighborhood in which locals can't afford to live. Who needs it?

Mark Halstead
Stop Rendezvous Coalition

1 Which statement best summarizes Cindy Koster's position?

A The best way to build a new school is to develop a ski area so more taxes will be generated.

B The new ski area will improve property values so people can sell their houses for more than they are worth now.

C The new ski area will provide economic and recreational benefits without harming the environment.

D The town is fine the way it is and doesn't need a new ski area.

2 On page 28 you learn that there will be a town <u>referendum</u>. What is a <u>referendum</u>?

F An election where people have a chance to vote on an issue

G A fiesta to celebrate an event such as the opening of the new ski area

H A meeting in which the developers seek the approval of the federal government

J A brochure describing what the ski area will look like

3 Who called Rendezvous Peak a "lodgepole pine desert"?

A Cindy Koster

B Mark Halstead

C Phoebe Blanchard

D A person who is not named

4 Which of these statements is an OPINION stated by Mark Halstead?

F The state will improve the highway.

G Outsiders will seek jobs at the ski area.

H Cutting the ski runs will remove about 5,000 acres of trees.

J Rendezvous Peak is not accessible now.

GO

Lesson 16: Test Yourself

5 From what you have read in this passage, you can conclude that —

  A forest fires have occurred often on Rendezvous Peak

  B there is no airport near the area where the ski slope is to be built

  C the economy in the region where the ski slope is to be built is good

  D the area where the slope is to be built is suffering through hard economic times

6 Cindy Koster quotes Phoebe Blanchard and indicates that her company, Environmental Designs, was hired by a government agency, the National Forest Service. Why do you think she presents this information?

  F So readers will know their tax dollars are being spent well by the National Forest Service.

  G So readers will believe the company is legitimate and unbiased.

  H The company has promised to improve the road if the ski area is developed.

  J Because the Forest Service will protect the environment.

7 Which of these statements is a FACT stated by Cindy Koster?

  A Rendezvous Peak will be the largest ski area in the state.

  B Everyone will enjoy the recreational opportunities provided by the ski area.

  C The ski area will generate more than $2,000,000 in tax revenues.

  D Everybody will benefit from Rendezvous Peak.

8 According to Phoebe Blanchard, the ski area will improve the environment. Which of these statements did she use to support her position?

  F Lodgepole pine will quickly take over the open ski runs.

  G The new plants that grow in the ski runs will be "oxygen engines."

  H Cutting the runs will encourage new plant species.

  J Forest fires are nature's way of revitalizing forests.

An Amazing Organ

The human eye is a truly amazing organ. It has the ability to translate reflected light from objects in the environment to signals that can be processed by the brain. And what is even more astounding, it does this by a simple yet effective process.

Light passes through the pupil or opening to the eye. It is then focused by the lens on the retina as an upside-down image. The image received by the retina is transmitted through the optic nerve to the brain where the image is "flipped" and interpreted.

The part of the eye that gives it color is called the iris. The iris, pupil, and lens are protected by a transparent covering called the cornea.

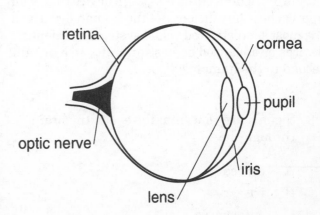

GO

Additional protection is given to the eye by the shape of the human face. The eye socket is set back slightly from the forehead and the cheekbones. As a result, injuries to the eye from large objects such as thrown balls are rare. The most obvious evidence of how well the shape of the head protects the eye is the number of "black eyes" that occur. Although painful and unsightly, a black eye is a small price to pay for an uninjured eye.

The eyelid is another layer of protection for the eye. Even though it seems flimsy, the eyelid is a tough cover that protects the eye from small and medium-sized objects like flying insects and blown dirt. The eyelid is controlled by a reflex reaction. A fast-moving object heading toward the eye will trigger the reflex and cause the eyelid to shut.

Tears are a fourth level of defense for the eye. They wash away small particles of dirt and dust that might damage the cornea. And each time you blink your eye, the eyelid lubricates the cornea with a new layer of tears that keeps the eye from drying out.

Even the pupil of the eye has a built-in safeguard. The pupil is designed to open and close according to how much light is available. If there is a sudden flash of light, for example, that might damage the retina, the pupil will quickly close as small as possible.

Scientists have studied the eye carefully in the hope of designing artificial vision systems for robots. Although they have made great strides, they are still far from developing a device that even approaches the efficiency of the human eye. Even the most sophisticated visual systems on scientific devices or advanced defense aircraft are a distant second to the human eye.

9 Signals are sent from the eye to the brain through the —

A cornea
B iris
C optic nerve
D retina

10 The word flimsy in this passage means —

F quick
G tough
H made of skin
J delicate

11 The lens is located —

A between the pupil and retina
B between the cornea and pupil
C below the optic nerve and retina
D on the outside of the cornea

12 When a doctor shines a light in your eye, the purpose is to see how well the eye reacts. What kind of reaction would the doctor expect from a bright light shining in your eye?

F The pupil should open.
G The pupil should close.
H The lens should close.
J The iris should open.

13 Which of these injuries is probably the most serious?

A A cut eyebrow
B A black eye
C A damaged retina
D A scratch on the eyelid

14 The lens of the eye can best be compared to which of these?

F An opening that can be adjusted
G A protective covering like a fingernail
H A movie screen
J An adjustable magnifying glass

STOP

Formulas

Perimeter of a square	$P = 4s$
Perimeter of a rectangle	$P = 2(l + w)$
Circumference of a circle	$C = 2\pi r$
Area of a square	$A = s^2$
Area of a rectangle	$A = l\,w$ or $A = bh$
Area of a triangle	$A = \dfrac{b\,h}{2}$
Area of a trapezoid	$A = \dfrac{1}{2}(b_1 + b_2)\,h$
Area of a circle	$A = \pi r^2$
Surface area of a cube	$S = 6\,s^2$
Surface area of a cylinder (lateral)	$S = 2\pi r\,h$
Volume of a rectangular prism	$V = l\,w\,h$
Volume of a cylinder	$V = \pi r^2\,h$
Volume of a cube	$V = s^3$
Pythagorean Theorem	$a^2 + b^2 = c^2$

Measurement Conversions

	METRIC	CUSTOMARY
Length	1 kilometer = 1000 meters	1 mile = 1760 yards
	1 meter = 100 centimeters	1 mile = 5280 feet
	1 centimeter = 10 millimeters	1 yard = 3 feet
		1 foot = 12 inches
Volume and Capacity	1 liter = 1000 milliliters	1 gallon = 4 quarts
		1 gallon = 128 ounces
		1 quart = 2 pints
		1 pint = 2 cups
		1 cup = 8 ounces
Weight and Mass	1 kilogram = 1000 grams	1 pound = 16 ounces
	1 gram = 1000 milligrams	1 ton = 2000 pounds
Time	1 year = 365 days	1 day = 24 hours
	1 year = 12 months	1 hour = 60 minutes
	1 year = 52 weeks	1 minute = 60 seconds
	1 week = 7 days	

GO

Lesson 17: Number Concepts

Samples   **Directions:** Read each mathematics problem. Mark the answer you think is correct.

A Which of the numbers below is <u>not</u> the same as the others?

A   one-eighth

B   12.5

C   12.5%

D $\frac{1}{8}$

B Which of these numbers shows the greatest distance?

F 6×10^{-8} cm

G 8×10^{-6} cm

H 9×10^{-3} cm

J 4×10^{-3} cm

Be sure to look at key words and numbers in both the problem and the answer choices.

Practice

1 How would you express the product $2 \times 2 \times 3 \times 3 \times 3 \times 4 \times 4$ using exponential notation?

A $2^2 \times 3^2 \times 4^2$

B $2^3 \times 3^4$

C $2^2 \times 3^2 \times 4^3$

D $2^2 \times 3^3 \times 4^2$

2 In a hardware store, pipe is stored in a rack with the smallest diameter on the bottom and the largest diameter on the top. Which of these would be on the top of the rack?

F $\frac{7}{10}$ in.

G $\frac{3}{4}$ in.

H $\frac{7}{8}$ in.

J $\frac{5}{8}$ in.

3 A map maker discovered that there was not enough room to write out a distance of 27.34 kilometers completely on a map. She decided to round the distance to the nearest tenth. Which of these distances did she use?

A   27.1 km

B   27.3 km

C   27.4 km

D   27.5 km

4 The sun is 93 million miles from the earth. How is this distance written using scientific notation?

F 9.3×10^7 miles

G 9.3×10^6 miles

H 9×10^3 miles

J 10^{93} miles

GO

Lesson 17: Number Concepts

5 A team of students measured the temperature of the soil in a garden at four times during the day. They discovered that the temperature increased steadily between 9:00 AM and 2:00 PM. Which of these answers shows the set of temperatures the students found?

A 84.01, 84.22, 84.19, 84.9

B 76.34, 76.2, 77.11, 77.08

C 78.01, 78.19, 78.62, 78.9

D 85.92, 85.88, 85.43, 85.12

6 The interest in Caitlin's bank account is computed at the rate of 5.58% per year. What is this rate expressed as a decimal?

F 55.8

G 5.58

H 0.558

J 0.0558

7 The diameter of the planet Jupiter is 88,640 miles. Which of these shows the diameter rounded to the nearest thousand?

A 90,000

B 89,000

C 86,000

D 80,000

8 Which of these is the same as $8^3 \cdot 3^2$?

F $8 \cdot 8 \cdot 8 \cdot 3 \cdot 3$

G $8 \cdot 3 \cdot 3 \cdot 2$

H $8 \cdot 8 \cdot 8 \cdot 2 \cdot 2$

J $8 \cdot 3 \cdot 3 \cdot 2 \cdot 2$

9 The price of cross-training shoes at four different stores was recently reduced. Advertisements for the stores showed how much the original price had been reduced. Which of these answers shows the greatest reduction?

A one-third

B 30%

C 0.024

D $\frac{1}{5}$

10 Which of these answer choices is closest in value to 2.3×10^2?

F 5.3×10^5

G 7.6×10^{-4}

H 9.1×10^2

J 2.8×10^{-2}

11 Each year, a greater proportion of students in a school pass an advanced placement test. The first year about one-quarter passed. During the second year, half of the students passed the test. The trend continued for a third year. Which of these shows the proportion of students who passed the test in the third year?

A $\frac{4}{5}$

B $\frac{3}{7}$

C $\frac{3}{8}$

D $\frac{2}{5}$

STOP

Lesson 18: Number Relations

Samples

Directions: Read each mathematics problem. Mark the answer you think is correct.

A What number will come next in the pattern shown below?

2, 5, 11, 23, ...

A 26

B 36

C 42

D 47

B Which answer falls within the range shown on this number line?

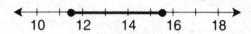

F 12.05

G 10.15

H 15.9

J 18.0

If you are not sure of the answer, take your best guess and go on to the next item.

Practice

1 What is the value of x in the expression shown below?

6x + 10 = 46

A 6

B 9

C 30

D 36

2 Which of these is equal to 5^4 ?

F $\dfrac{2^5}{3^5}$

G $\dfrac{2^6}{3^2}$

H $\dfrac{5^4}{4^5}$

J $\dfrac{5^6}{5^2}$

3 Which point below is nearest (4, 5)?

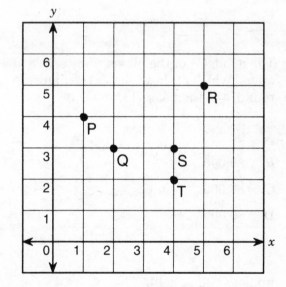

A Q

B R

C S

D T

GO

Lesson 18: Number Relations

4 Which of these answers is <u>not</u> equal to

$$3 \times (5 - 2)$$

F   (3 x 5) – (3 x 2)

G   9

H   (3 x 5) – 2

J   (5 – 2) x 3

7 A research team studied a 36-acre plot of land. They found that an average of 9 hawks hunted there each day. The researchers also found an average of 81 snakes a day on the plot. What was the ratio of hawks to snakes?

A   1 to 9

B   1 to 4

C   4 to 9

D   9 to 1

Use this graph to answer questions 5 and 6.

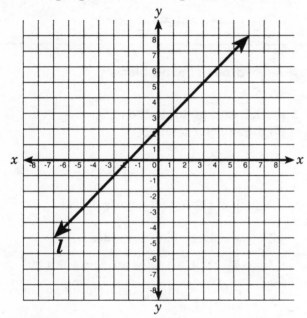

5 Which of these is an equation of line *l* ?

A   y = x + 3

B   y = x + 2

C   y = x – 2

D   y = 2(x)

6 What is the value of y when x is equal to -4?

F   2

G   0

H   -2

J   -6

8 A car dealer determines the price she will charge for a car by using the formula:

$$P = (C \times 1.1) + T$$

where P is the price she will charge, C is the cost paid to the manufacturer, and T is a transportation fee. What will the price of a car be if it costs the dealer $12,000 and the transportation fee is $275.00?

F $13,200.00

G $13,275.00

H $13,475.00

J $13,502.50

9 In which of these is n equal to 5?

A   7n + 8 = 29

B $\frac{4}{5}$ n + 8 = 12

C $\frac{2}{5}$ n + 16 = 20

D   5n – 8 = 42

STOP

Sample

Directions: Read each geometry problem. Mark the answer you think is correct.

A For which of these figures is Area $= \frac{bh}{2}$?

A

B

C

D

Look at each figure carefully and use key words in the problem to help you find the answer.

If you know which answer is correct, mark it and go on to the next item. You do not have to look at all the answer choices.

Practice

1 In the illustration below, the transformation from Figure A to Figure B involves —

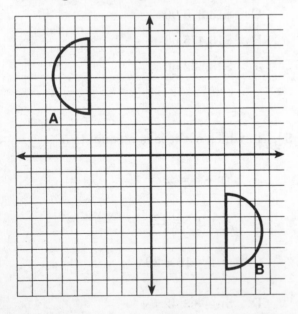

A rotation and translation

B reflection and rotation

C reflection and translation

D translation and deflection

2 Which of these statements is true?

F A polygon has five sides.

G All obtuse angles are less than 90°.

H Rotation and translation mean the same thing.

J A line of symmetry divides a figure into two identical parts.

3 Look at the answer choices below. Which of them is a ray?

A

B

C

D

GO

4 Look at the figure below. It shows how to —

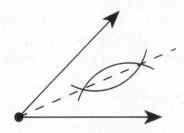

F construct an angle bisector

G determine the arc of a circle

H calculate the size of an angle

J construct a perpendicular bisector of a line segment

5 The illustration below shows the course for a triathlon. How could you find the distance of the canoe part of the race?

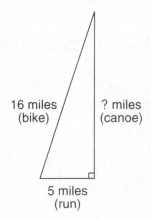

16 miles (bike)   ? miles (canoe)

5 miles (run)

A $16^2 - 5^2$

B $\sqrt{16^2 - 5^2}$

C $\sqrt{5^2 - 16^2}$

D $\sqrt{16^2 + 5^2}$

6 Which of these statements is false?

F All circles are similar.

G All squares are similar.

H All right triangles are similar.

J All equilateral triangles are similar.

7 The figure below shows a square with sides of 1 unit and a diagonal equal to the square root of 2. Based on your knowledge of squares, triangles, and the figure below, you can conclude that —

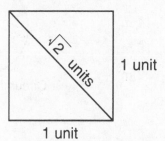

1 unit

1 unit

A the diagonal of any square can be found by adding the length of the sides to the square root of 2

B the diagonal of any square can be found by multiplying the length of the sides by the square root of 2

C the length of the sides will be less than the square root of 2

D the diagonal will always be the square root of 2

8 The two triangles below are similar. If the length of the missing side of the larger triangle is 22, what is the length of the missing side of the smaller triangle?

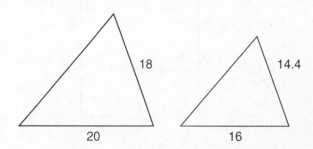

18   14.4

20   16

F 26.4

G 20

H 18

J 17.6

STOP

Lesson 20: Measurement

Sample

Directions: Read each measurement problem. Mark the answer you think is correct.

A What is the radius of this circle? Use $\pi = \frac{22}{7}$

- **A** 7 m
- **B** 14 m
- **C** 15 m
- **D** 22 m

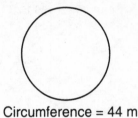

Circumference = 44 m

B A recipe that serves 4 people calls for 10 ounces of chicken. How many **pounds** of chicken would you need to serve 16 people?

- **F** 1 pound
- **G** $1\frac{1}{4}$ pounds
- **H** $2\frac{1}{2}$ pounds
- **J** 3 pounds

Before you try to choose an answer, be sure you know what the question is asking.

Look for key words such as *perimeter*, *circumference*, *area*, and *volume*.

Practice

1 A piece of wall board is 4 feet wide by 6 feet long. A carpenter cut the shape below out of a piece of wall board. What is the area of the remaining piece of wall board?

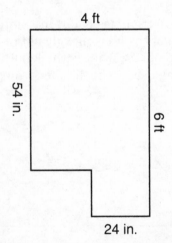

4 ft

54 in.

6 ft

24 in.

- **A** 24 in.²
- **B** 32 in.²
- **C** 78 in.²
- **D** 432 in.²

2 A standard basketball goal is about how high?

- **F** 3 m
- **G** 3 ft
- **H** 300 in.
- **J** 30 yd

3 A swimming pool is 50 yards long, 20 yards wide, and 2 yards deep. How much water will be needed to fill the pool?

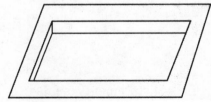

- **A** 20,000 yds³
- **B** 2000 yds³
- **C** 1000 yds³
- **D** 280 yds³

GO

Lesson 20: Measurement

4   Look at the section of a ruler shown below. What is the greatest precision that can be achieved with this ruler?

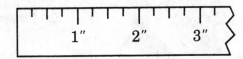

F   Nearest 1 inch

G   Nearest $\frac{3}{4}$ inch

H   Nearest $\frac{1}{2}$ inch

J   Nearest $\frac{1}{4}$ inch

5   Which of these is the greatest distance?

A   2000 feet

B   1000 yards

C $\frac{1}{4}$ mile

D   1 kilometer

6   Which statement about the figure below is true?

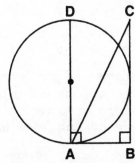

F $\overline{AD} = \overline{AC}$

G $\overline{AC} < \overline{AB}$

H $\overline{AB}$ is equal to the radius of the circle.

J $\overline{AD}$ is equal to the radius of the circle.

7   How would you find the volume of this cylinder?

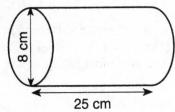

A $\frac{22}{7}$ x 400 cm^3

B $\frac{22}{7}$ x 400 cm^3

C $\frac{22}{7}$ x 1600 cm^3

D $\frac{22}{7}$ x 6400 cm^3

8   A container holds 1 liter of water. You pour 350 mL of water from the container into a glass. How much water is left in the container?

F   50 mL

G   500 mL

H   650 mL

J   750 mL

9   What is the area of this parallelogram?

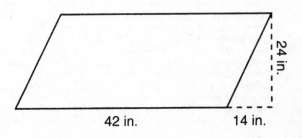

A   336 in.^{2}

B   1008 in.^{2}

C   1022 in.^{2}

D   14,112 in.^{2}

STOP

Lesson 21: Probability and Statistics

Sample

Directions: Read each mathematics problem. Mark the answer you think is correct.

A This wheel shows 4 different prizes you can win. If you spin the wheel just once, what prize are you most likely to win?

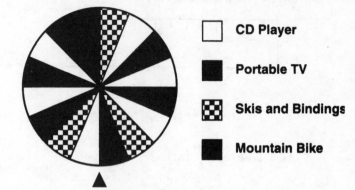

- ☐ CD Player
- ■ Portable TV
- ▨ Skis and Bindings
- ■ Mountain Bike

A Portable TV

B Skis and Bindings

C Mountain Bike

D CD Player

If you work on scratch paper, be sure to transfer numbers correctly from the problem to the scratch paper. Work carefully, and if the answer you find is not one of the answer choices, work the problem again.

Practice

1 Evita is planning her school schedule. She referred to the chart below and found the number of sections of math, English, and science. Each section is taught by a different teacher. She plans to take one section of each subject. How many different combinations of these three courses might she consider?

Math 1	Math 2	Math 3	
English 1	English 2	English 3	English 4
Reading 1	Reading 2	Reading 3	Reading 4
History 1	History 2	History 3	History 4
Science 1	Science 2	Science 3	
Writing 1	Writing 2	Writing 3	Writing 4

A 48

B 36

C 10

D 3

2 There are 5 pairs of gloves in a ski bag. Suppose you picked one glove at a time out of the bag without looking. How many times would you have to pick before you were sure you had a pair of gloves?

F 2 times

G 4 times

H 5 times

J 6 times

3 Raoul's scores on 4 tests were 83, 86, 80, and 81. He has one more test to take, and he wants to earn an 85 average in the class. What score must he get to have an 85 average?

A 85

B 90

C 95

D 96

GO

Lesson 21: Probability and Statics

This graph shows a family's monthly electric bills. Use this graph to answer questions 4 through 6.

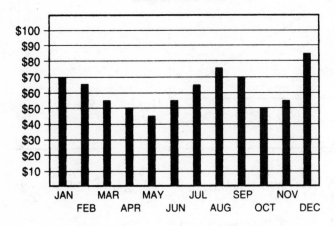

ELECTRIC BILL

4 What is the mode of the amounts shown on the graph?

   F $50

   G $55

   H $60

   J $65

5 What is the range of the amounts shown on the graph?

   A $45 to $65

   B $50 to $85

   C $55 to $80

   D $45 to $85

6 What is the mean (average) of the amounts paid in December, January, February, and March?

   F $68.75

   G $68.00

   H $63.75

   J $63.00

7 Each month, 1 student is chosen from a class of 25 students to be the representative to student council. How would you calculate the probability of the same student being chosen as class representative for 2 months in a row?

   A $\frac{1}{25}$ x 2

   B $\frac{1}{25}$ x $\frac{1}{2}$

   C $\frac{1}{25}$ x $\frac{1}{25}$

   D $\frac{1}{25}$ x $\frac{25}{1}$

This chart shows the month of birth for the students in a class. Use the chart to answer question 8.

Month of Birth	Number of Students
January	/ /
February	/ /
March	/ /
April	/ / /
May	/ /
June	/
July	/ / / / /
August	/ /
September	/ / / /
October	/ /
November	/ / /
December	/ /

8 What is the mode for this frequency distribution?

   F 3

   G 4

   H 5

   J 6

STOP

Lesson 22: Test Yourself

Sample A

What is the area of triangle ABD?

A 84 units ^{2}

B 42 units ^{2}

C 35 units ^{2}

D 17.5 units ^{2}

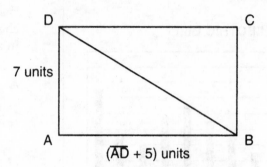

7 units

($\overline{AD}$ + 5) units

---

1 The picture frame below is 2 meters high by 3 meters wide. What is the perimeter of the frame in centimeters?

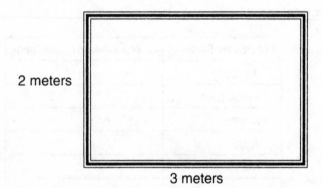

2 meters

3 meters

A 6 cm

B 10 cm

C 100 cm

D 1000 cm

2 A liter is equal to 0.0353 cubic feet. How would you express this number using scientific notation?

F 3.53×10^{-2} ft ^{3}

G 35.3×10^{-4} ft ^{3}

H 353×10^{-5} ft ^{3}

J 3.53×10^{2} ft ^{3}

3 Which equation is equivalent to 5T + 6 = 21?

A $5(T + 6) = 21$

B $2(5T + 6) = 21 \div 2$

C $5T + 6 - 8 = 21 - 8$

D $3(T - 2) + 6 = 21$

4 What is the area of the circle shown below? Use π = 3.14.

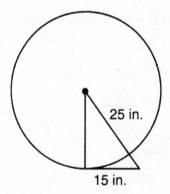

25 in.

15 in.

F 1962.5 units²

G 1256 units²

H 706.5 units²

J 125.6 units²

GO

Lesson 22: Test Yourself

5 What is the value of **a** in this equation?

$$6(a + 8) = 63$$

A 3

B 3.5

C 2.5

D 2

Use this figure to answer questions 6 and 7.

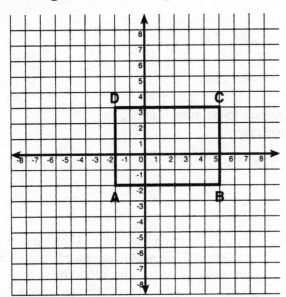

6 What shape would you have if you moved corners D and C two units to the left?

F rectangle

G trapezoid

H square

J parallelogram

7 What is the area of the shape shown above?

A 36 units²

B 35 units²

C 24 units²

D 12 units²

8 Which of these is about 0.8 yards wide?

F a doorway

G a garage

H an envelope

J an airplane

9 Sue and Marty were comparison shopping for sunglasses. The most expensive glasses they found were $49.95. They found the same glasses for $11 less at a discount store. Which number line shows this range of prices?

A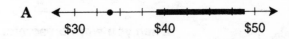

B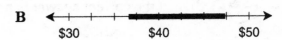

C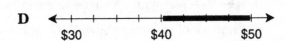

D
$30 $40 $50

10 Which number should come next in this pattern?

$$2\frac{1}{10}, 4\frac{1}{5}, 8\frac{3}{10}, \dots$$

F $12\frac{7}{10}$

G $16\frac{2}{5}$

H $16\frac{7}{10}$

J $18\frac{2}{5}$

STOP

ANSWER ROWS   **5** Ⓐ Ⓑ Ⓒ Ⓓ   **6** Ⓕ Ⓖ Ⓗ Ⓙ   **7** Ⓐ Ⓑ Ⓒ Ⓓ
8 Ⓕ Ⓖ Ⓗ Ⓙ   **9** Ⓐ Ⓑ Ⓒ Ⓓ   **10** Ⓕ Ⓖ Ⓗ Ⓙ   Number Correct_____   **53**

Samples

Directions: Read each addition problem. Mark the answer you think is correct.

A Ray earns about $500 a week. He pays 15% in federal taxes, 2.6% in state taxes, and 7.5% in other taxes. He also has 5% of each paycheck transferred to a retirement account. What is the total percentage of Ray's paycheck that goes to taxes?

A 15%

B 22.5%

C 25.7%

D 27.5%

E Not Here

B How long will a runway be if it is now $\frac{7}{8}$ of a mile long and you extend it by $\frac{1}{4}$ of a mile?

F $1\frac{1}{8}$ miles

G $1\frac{1}{4}$ miles

H $1\frac{4}{7}$ miles

J $1\frac{7}{8}$ miles

K Not Here

When you work on scratch paper, check to be sure that digits and decimal points are lined up correctly.

If the correct answer is not shown, choose "Not Here."

Practice

1 A picture window is $8\frac{1}{3}$ feet wide. On each side of the window there is a section of drapes $2\frac{3}{4}$ feet wide. A carpenter wants to put a piece of molding above the window and both drapes. How long must the piece of molding be?

A $10\frac{1}{8}$ feet

B $10\frac{3}{4}$ feet

C $12\frac{5}{6}$ feet

D $13\frac{5}{6}$ feet

E Not Here

2 A stadium currently holds 4598 fans. A new section of 2785 seats was recently added, and 6920 seats will be added next year. How many people in all will the stadium hold after next year?

F 15,303

G 14,303

H 11,518

J 7383

K Not Here

3 A pumpkin weighs 15.67 kilograms. How much will it weigh if it gains 1.08 kilograms in one week and 2.2 kilograms the next?

A 18.95 kg

B 18.77 kg

C 18.75 kg

D 16.75 kg

E 15.95

GO

Lesson 23: Addition

4 The census report for a county showed that 12.88% of the adults leased automobiles and 82.9% owned them. The same report showed that 57.34% of the adults lived in a home they owned singly or jointly, and that 36.91% lived in a home they rented. What was the total percentage of adults who owned or leased automobiles?

F 84.25%

G 94.25%

H 94.78%

J 95.78%

K Not Here

5 The Kansas Turnpike is 233 miles long, the New York Thruway is 496 miles long, and the Pennsylvania Turnpike is 358 miles long. How long are these three turnpikes all together?

A 729 miles

B 854 miles

C 987 miles

D 1088 miles

E Not here

6 The members of a bicycle club are planning a trip. They will bike for $6\frac{2}{3}$ hours on the first day, 8 on the second day, $5\frac{1}{2}$ on the third day, and $3\frac{5}{6}$ on the fourth day. What is the total time they will spend biking?

F 16 hours

G $22\frac{4}{7}$ hours

H $22\frac{7}{12}$ hours

J $23\frac{5}{6}$ hours

K 24 hours

7 A business recently bought a new computer system. The computer itself cost $1845, and the software cost $679. The service contract was $180 per year, and a special backup power supply was $918. How much did the business pay for the computer, software, and power supply?

A $3622

B $3442

C $2943

D $1777

E Not Here

8 A box is $30\frac{1}{4}$ inches long, $18\frac{5}{8}$ inches wide, and $14\frac{1}{16}$ inches deep. You want to tape the box closed, but have just a little tape left. What is the shortest length of tape that will go around the box?

F $56\frac{1}{4}$ in.

G $64\frac{7}{8}$ in.

H $65\frac{3}{8}$ in.

J $98\frac{1}{4}$ in.

K Not Here

9 A space station is 1229 miles from earth. A satellite is 3387 miles from the space station. How far is the satellite from earth?

A 2158 miles

B 4616 miles

C 4618 miles

D 5616 miles

E 15,677 miles

STOP

Samples   **Directions:** Read each subtraction problem. Mark the answer you think is correct.

A Kelly bought a sweater for $54.95, less a "good customer" discount of $15.29. What did she pay for the sweater?

    A $39.64

    B $39.66

    C $49.64

    D $49.66

    E Not Here

B What will be left if you cut $4\frac{3}{8}$ feet off a board 12 feet long?

    F $6\frac{3}{8}$ ft

    G $6\frac{5}{8}$ ft

    H $7\frac{5}{8}$ ft

    J $16\frac{3}{8}$ ft

    K Not Here

When you subtract fractions, rewrite the numbers carefully on scratch paper in a form that lets you work easily.

If you are not sure of an answer, check it by adding.

Practice

1 For three weeks, a worker earned $456.78, $399.25, and $465.66. What was the difference between the highest and lowest amounts she earned?

    A $8.88

    B $57.53

    C $66.51

    D $149.95

    E Not Here

2 The barometric pressure at 8:00 AM was 29.58 in. Hg. It rose to 30.06 in. Hg by 3:00 PM. How much did the pressure rise during the day?

    F 0.48 in. Hg

    G 0.52 in. Hg

    H 0.64 in. Hg

    J 0.68 in. Hg

    K Not Here

3 In order to buy a custom-made screen, Dennis had to take three measurements of the width of the door. The measurements were $30\frac{15}{16}$, $31\frac{3}{16}$, and $31\frac{1}{4}$ inches. How far apart were the two closest measurements he took?

    A $\frac{1}{16}$ in.

    B $\frac{1}{8}$ in.

    C $\frac{1}{4}$ in.

    D $1\frac{1}{16}$ in.

    E $1\frac{1}{8}$ in.

GO

Lesson 24: Subtraction

4 The odometer on a rental car read 6921 after a round trip to Oklahoma. The odometer at the beginning of the trip was 5077. How far was the round trip?

F 844 miles

G 1845 miles

H 1855 miles

J 1944 miles

K Not Here

5 In order to be promoted, a worker needs 15 productivity points. The worker's point total in October was $10\frac{3}{4}$ and increased in November to $12\frac{5}{16}$. How many more productivity points does the worker still need to be promoted?

A $3\frac{11}{16}$ points

B $2\frac{11}{16}$ points

C $2\frac{9}{16}$ points

D $2\frac{1}{8}$ points

E Not Here

6 Water boils at 212°F and alcohol boils at 148°F. The temperature of a container of unknown liquid is 76.55°F. How much more would you have to raise the temperature of the liquid to discover if it was alcohol?

F 71.45°F

G 71.55°F

H 72.45°F

J 72.55°F

K 135.45°F

7 The students in a school were having a fund raiser to buy a camcorder. They raised $559. The camcorder they wanted cost $799, but the store owner said she would let them have it for $50 less. How much more money did the students have to raise?

A $180

B $190

C $199

D $240

E Not Here

8 A piece of aluminum is being prepared for use in the space shuttle. It is now 0.14 mm thick, but it is only supposed to be 0.127 mm thick. How much aluminum must be ground from the piece so it is the correct thickness?

F 0.113 mm

G 0.27 mm

H 0.22 mm

J 0.12 mm

K Not Here

9 One truck carries $19\frac{5}{9}$ tons of dirt and another carries $21\frac{4}{9}$ tons. The first truck dumps its dirt into a hole but doesn't fill it. The second truck dumps $4\frac{5}{9}$ tons of dirt and fills the hole. How much dirt is left in the second truck?

A $24\frac{1}{9}$ tons

B $16\frac{8}{9}$ tons

C $16\frac{1}{9}$ tons

D 16 tons

E 15 tons

STOP

Test Prep ANSWER ROWS **4** Ⓕ Ⓖ Ⓗ Ⓙ Ⓚ   **5** Ⓐ Ⓑ Ⓒ Ⓓ Ⓔ   **6** Ⓕ Ⓖ Ⓗ Ⓙ Ⓚ
7 Ⓐ Ⓑ Ⓒ Ⓓ Ⓔ   **8** Ⓕ Ⓖ Ⓗ Ⓙ Ⓚ   **9** Ⓐ Ⓑ Ⓒ Ⓓ Ⓔ

Lesson 25: Multiplication

Samples   **Directions:** Read each multiplication problem. Mark the answer you think is correct.

A A teacher bases students' grades on a total of 750 points. The final exam is worth 24% of a student's grade. How many points is the final exam worth?

    A   180

    B   314

    C   726

    D   774

    E   Not Here

B Cecelia needed 25 copies of a 7 page report. The copy center charges $.08 per page, so each report will cost $.56. How much will it cost Cecelia to make 25 copies of the report?

    F $4.48

    G $5.60

    H $12.00

    J $14.00

    K $28.00

If necessary, work the problem on scratch paper. Be sure to copy the numbers correctly when you do.

After you have found an answer, ask yourself: "Does this answer make sense?"

Practice

1 Reggie is helping his parents build a deck. He must cut 8 boards each to a length of $6\frac{1}{3}$ feet. What will the total length of these boards be when he finishes cutting them?

    A   60 feet

    B $50\frac{2}{3}$ feet

    C   48 feet

    D $48\frac{1}{3}$ feet

    E   Not Here

2 A round-trip plane ticket from Dallas to Phoenix costs $149. How much will it cost a college if 36 football players fly from Dallas to Phoenix and back?

    F $185

    G $4364

    H $5362

    J $5363

    K   Not Here

3 If 1 gallon of water weighs 8.3 pounds, how much will 2.45 gallons of water weigh?

    A   11.75 pounds

    B   10.335 pounds

    C   19.335 pounds

    D   20.335 pounds

    E   Not Here

GO

Lesson 25: Multiplication

4 A company that sells books ships 175 cases of books each week. A case holds 18 books and weighs 54 pounds. How many pounds of books does the company ship in a week?

F 247 pounds

G 972 pounds

H 9540 pounds

J 9570 pounds

K Not Here

5 A truck delivered 28 pieces of pipe to a drilling site. Each piece of pipe was $22\frac{1}{4}$ feet long. How many feet of pipe were delivered by the truck?

A 623 ft

B $623\frac{1}{4}$ ft

C $672\frac{1}{4}$ ft

D 676 ft

E Not Here

6 Evaporation causes the loss of 0.39 mm of water from a lake each day. How many millimeters of water does the pond lose through evaporation in 90 days?

F 39.9 mm

G 36.1 mm

H 36.01 mm

J 35.1 mm

K 35.01 mm

7 A ninth grade class at a local school adopted a section of highway. They pick up litter on the highway once each month. To do this, they walk an average of $5\frac{3}{8}$ miles each month. How many miles of highway do they walk in a year?

A $60\frac{3}{8}$ miles

B $64\frac{1}{2}$ miles

C $64\frac{3}{8}$ miles

D 68 miles

E Not Here

8 A container of chemicals is 0.98 meters tall. In the warehouse, the containers are normally stacked 10 high. What is the total distance from the floor of the warehouse to the top of the seventh container on the stack?

F 9.8 m

G 7.98 m

H 6.86 m

J 6.02 m

K 5.02 m

9 A garden store sells potted daisies for $3.49 each. How much will it cost to buy 16 of them?

A $39.49

B $48.49

C $54.84

D $55.84

E Not Here

STOP

Lesson 26: Division

Samples

Directions: Read each division problem. Mark the answer you think is correct.

A A cantaloupe weighs 3.12 pounds. It was divided into 4 pieces. How much does each piece weigh?

   A   12.48 pounds

   B   7.12 pounds

   C   0.88 pounds

   D   0.78 pounds

   E   Not Here

B A shipper bought 1895 pounds of potatoes for $.06 a pound. How many 50-pound bags can the shipper fill with the potatoes?

   F   113.7 bags

   G   56 bags

   H   50.06 bags

   J   39.7 bags

   K   Not Here

Remember, you can check your answer by multiplying.

Be careful! Some problems contain numbers that are not needed to solve the problem.

Practice

1 A school library has 833 fiction books. There are an average of 17 books per shelf. How many shelves of fiction books are in the library?

   A   56

   B   49

   C   48.17

   D   39

   E   Not Here

2 A town of 3755 has 7 doctors and 4 dentists. What is the average number of people each dentist serves, rounded to the nearest whole number?

   F   341

   G   275

   H   536

   J   839

   K   939

3 A box of blank video tapes costs $36.64. If one tape costs $2.29, how many tapes are in a box?

   A   36

   B   34

   C   17

   D   12

   E   Not Here

4 A flooring tile is 9 inches on each side, so each tile has a surface area of 81 square inches. How many tiles would be needed to cover a bathroom floor that is 7776 square inches?

   F   90

   G   96

   H   729

   J   864

   K   Not Here

GO

Lesson 26: Division

5 A homeowner burns 142.5 cubic feet of wood every 30 days. The homeowner spends about 25 minutes a day tending the fire. How much wood does the homeowner burn in one day?

A 4.7 cubic feet

B 4.75 cubic feet

C 5 cubic feet

D 5.7 cubic feet

E 5.75 cubic feet

6 An apartment building houses 250 people living in 80 apartments. The building is 10 stories tall. What is the average number of people in each apartment?

F 25

G 8

H 3.125

J 2.625

K Not Here

7 It takes $2\frac{1}{3}$ pounds of seed to fill a bird feeder. The birds empty the feeder in about 3 days. If there are 50 pounds of seed in a bag, how many times will you be able to fill a feeder from 1 bag?

A $116\frac{2}{3}$

B $116\frac{1}{3}$

C 22

D $21\frac{3}{7}$

E Not Here

8 How many 4.4-ounce bottles of glue could you fill from a container that holds 140.8 ounces?

F 32

G 32.4

H 34

J 34.4

K 35.2

9 A herd of cattle travels about $31\frac{1}{2}$ miles in a day. The cowboys who drive the cattle work 10-hour days, but the cattle walk for only 9 hours a day. How far do the cattle move in an hour?

A 4 miles

B $3\frac{1}{3}$ miles

C $2\frac{1}{2}$ miles

D 2 miles

E Not Here

10 A storage freezer has a volume of 394.4 cubic feet and an area of 49 square feet. It is filled with 68 cases of frozen fruit. Each case contains 12 packages of frozen fruit. How many cubic feet does each case hold?

F 80

G 8.04

H 6

J 5.8

K Not Here

STOP

Lesson 27: Test Yourself

Sample A

Water freezes at 32°F. If the temperature is at 51°F, how far must it drop before ice forms on a pond?

A   83°F

B   32°F

C   18°F

D   16°F

E   Not Here

Sample B

If a gallon of milk costs $2.25, how much will it cost to buy 18 gallons of milk for a Labor Day picnic?

F $15.75

G $20.25

H $40.50

J $42.50

K   Not Here

---

1   It snowed in north Texas for 4 days in a row. The amounts were $2\frac{1}{2}$ inches, $4\frac{1}{4}$ inches, $3\frac{5}{8}$ inches, and $7\frac{1}{3}$ inches. How much snow fell in all during the 4-day period?

A $18\frac{7}{24}$ inches

B   18 inches

C $17\frac{17}{24}$ inches

D $16\frac{3}{8}$ inches

E   Not Here

2   The bus route from the center of a city to the mall is 29.72 miles. The route from the mall to the airport is 32.64. How much farther is the second trip than the first?

F   62.36 miles

G   32.72 miles

H   3.92 miles

J   2.92 miles

K   2.12 miles

3   What would the total bill be if you bought a watch for $29.95, a sweater for $39.95, socks for $9.95, and a wallet for $19.95?

A $99.85

B $99.80

C $89.85

D $70.00

E $9.98

4   A mail order business calculates the percentage of its annual business for each month of the year. In September it does 4.8%, in October 5.93%, in November 14.04%, and in December 28.56%. What is the total percentage of business it does during the months of October, November, and December?

F   38.53%

G   42.6%

H   52.33%

J   53.33%

K   Not here

GO

ANSWER ROWS   **A** Ⓐ Ⓑ Ⓒ Ⓓ Ⓔ   **B** Ⓕ Ⓖ Ⓗ Ⓙ Ⓚ   **1** Ⓐ Ⓑ Ⓒ Ⓓ Ⓔ

2 Ⓕ Ⓖ Ⓗ Ⓙ Ⓚ   **3** Ⓐ Ⓑ Ⓒ Ⓓ Ⓔ   **4** Ⓕ Ⓖ Ⓗ Ⓙ Ⓚ

Test Prep

5 A boat is traveling at a speed of $15\frac{3}{4}$ miles an hour. Its maximum speed is 24 miles an hour. How long will it take to travel 2782 miles if it was traveling at its maximum speed?

A $16\frac{3}{4}$ hours

B $14\frac{1}{4}$ hours

C 14 hours

D $9\frac{1}{4}$ hours

E Not Here

6 In 1968, Tommie Smith won the 200-meter run in the Olympics with a time of 19.83 seconds. The Olympic winner in 1988, Jo DeLoach, won with a time of 19.75. How much faster was DeLoach's time?

F 0.08 seconds

G 0.18 seconds

H 0.19 seconds

J 39.58 seconds

K Not Here

7 A student works 2 hours a day during the summer for 21 days a month. Each day, the student earns $8.56. How much does the student earn each hour?

A $10.56

B $10.50

C $6.56

D $4.33

E $4.28

8 In a relay race, the times of the four runners on a team were 10.03 seconds, 9.98 seconds, 9.72 seconds, and 10.16 seconds. What was the total time for this team?

F 30.08 seconds

G 39.089 seconds

H 39.89 seconds

J 40.089 seconds

K 40.89 seconds

9 A chair lift at a ski area can carry 4 skiers in each chair. It takes $19\frac{4}{5}$ minutes for a chair to go from the bottom to the top and back again. How many chairs are needed to carry 296 skiers to the top of the mountain?

A $73\frac{4}{5}$

B 74

C $84\frac{1}{5}$

D 84

E Not Here

10 Roxanne runs 3.25 miles a day. She runs Monday through Friday, but not on Saturday or Sunday. How far does she run each week?

F 22.75 miles

G 22 miles

H 16.525 miles

J 16.25 miles

K 15.125 miles

STOP

Lesson 28: Estimation

Samples   **Directions:** Read each mathematics problem. Mark the answer you think is correct.

A On a baseball diamond, it is 90 feet between bases. About how far does someone run who hits a home run?

    A 90 feet

    B 200 feet

    C between 200 and 250 feet

    D between 250 and 300 feet

    E between 350 and 400 feet

B Plane A travels 25% faster than plane B. If a trip takes plane B an hour, about how long will it take plane A to make the trip?

    F 15 minutes

    G 30 minutes

    H 45 minutes

    J 1 hour and 15 minutes

    K 90 minutes

For some problems, there is no exact answer. If you have worked a problem on scratch paper and found an answer that is not one of the answer choices, select the answer choice that is closest to your answer.

Practice

1 Suppose that the scale on a map indicates that 1 inch = 10 miles. About how far apart would two towns be if they were 6.65 inches apart on the map?

    A 6.5 miles

    B 60 miles

    C 65 miles

    D 70 miles

    E 650 miles

2 A computer technician charges $25 an hour, plus a service call charge of $15. About how much would her bill be if she spent 3 hours and 15 minutes fixing the computer in an office?

    F $25

    G about $40

    H between $50 and $75

    J about $100

    K between $100 and $125

3 A pair of tennis shoes costing $50 goes on sale for 20% off the regular price. After the sale, the store raises the price 20%. About how much do the tennis shoes cost now?

    A between $40 and $45

    B between $45 and $50

    C $50

    D between $50 and $55

    E $60

4 What is the total thickness of 8 boards if each board is 0.89 inches thick?

    F between 1 and 2 inches

    G between 2 and 6 inches

    H about 6 inches

    J between 6.5 and 7 inches

    K about 7 inches

GO

5 There are 514 students in a school. Two of the students are running for student council president. Only half the students in the school voted, and of these, 106 voted for candidate A. About how many students voted for candidate B?

   A less than 50

   B between 50 and 90

   C about 100

   D between 100 and 140

   E about 150

6 Freddy had $30 to spend for a picnic. He spent $17.75 on food. With the rest of the money, he bought bottles of juice. If juice costs $1.95 a bottle, about how many bottles of juice did he buy?

   F 6

   G 7

   H 9

   J 11

   K 12

7 Jerry and 3 of her friends went to lunch. Each spent about $4. When they received the bill, it was for $19.86. Jerry told the waiter he had made a mistake in adding. About how far off was he from the correct amount?

   A $16

   B $13

   C $8

   D $4

   E $1

8 The daily flight from El Paso to Dallas carries an average of 91 passengers. The airline reduced the price of tickets for a week and found that the average number of passengers increased by 10%. About how many more passengers flew during the 7-day week with reduced prices than during a week of regular prices?

   F about 10

   G about 50

   H about 60

   J about 600

   K about 700

9 The average temperature in a city is 31° in January and 68° in May. Assume that the temperature increases about the same amount each month. What will the average temperature be in the month of March?

   A about 35°

   B about 40°

   C about 45°

   D about 50°

   E about 60°

10 The monthly electric bills for a small business for 5 months were $81.25, $89.86, $86.05, $67.99, and $74.54. The owner of the business believes the bills for the rest of the year will show the same pattern. About how much will the owner of the business pay in a year for electricity?

   F more than $1000

   G between $900 and $1000

   H between $900 and $9000

   J between $700 and $8000

   K less than $700

STOP

Sample   **Directions:** Read each mathematics problem. Mark the answer you think is correct.

A Look at this figure. A and C are the centers of two circles. Point B is on the circumference of both circles. If AB = 2BC, what is the diameter of a circle with center A if C is on its circumference?

A 2πAC

B 2πBC

C AB + BC

D AC

E 6BC

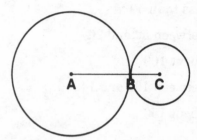

Read the question carefully and think about what you are supposed to do. Don't be confused by numbers or parts of figures that are not necessary to solve the problem.

Practice

1 A cord of wood is 8 feet long, 4 feet high, and 4 feet deep. How many logs are needed to make a cord if a log is 16 feet long and the surface area of a cut through the log averages 1 square foot?

A 16 logs

B 12.8 logs

C 9 logs

D 8 logs

E Not Here

2 A baseball player's batting average is .250. How many hits would you expect the player to get if she comes to bat 88 times?

F 25

G 23

H 12

J 11

K Not Here

3 An artist is planning to cut a mat to go around a picture. The shaded portion of the figure below shows the area of the mat. How can you calculate the area of the mat?

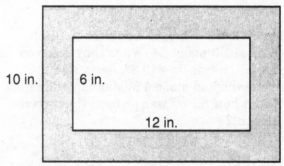

10 in.   6 in.   12 in.   16 in.

A (16 x 10) – (12 x 6)

B (2•10 + 2•16) – (2•6 + 2•12)

C (16 x 10) + (12 x 6)

D (12•16) – (6•10)

E (12•16) + (6•10)

GO

4   Suppose you tried each of these spinners just once. On which one would you most likely land on 1?

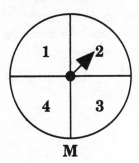

M

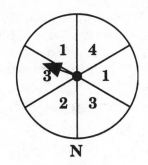

N

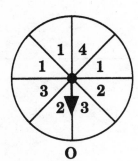

O

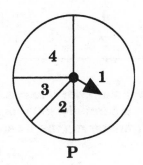

P

F   M

G   N

H   O

J   P

K   You would have the same chance on all of them.

5   This chart shows the test scores for 8 students. The students are identified by their initials. What would the average score for the class be if the score of student OP increased to 96?

Students	BR	SS	OP	TR	DC	GR	LJ	JB
Scores	80	85	88	94	78	84	91	92

A   94.5

B   92

C   87.6

D   86.8

E   Not Here

6   How could you find the speed at which the earth is rotating on its axis if you know the diameter of the earth is about 7900 miles?

F $\dfrac{7900 \times \pi}{24}$

G $\dfrac{3950^2 \times \pi}{24}$

H $\dfrac{7900 \times \pi^2}{24}$

J $\dfrac{3950 \times \pi}{24}$

K $\dfrac{7900 \times 24}{\pi}$

7   A farmer usually plants 2000 acres a year. This year, he planted 800 acres of cotton, 400 acres of sorghum, and 200 acres of soy beans. He didn't plant anything in the remaining acres because of financial problems. How can you find the percentage of planted acreage that went to cotton?

A $\dfrac{400}{800 + 400 + 200}$

B $\dfrac{2000 - 800}{2000}$

C $\dfrac{800}{2000}$

D $\dfrac{2000 - 400 - 200}{800 + 400 + 200}$

E $\dfrac{800}{800 + 400 + 200}$

8   There are 450 students in a school, and 234 of them are girls. If the number of students in the school increases to 525 and the percentage of girls remains the same, how many girls will be in the school?

F   216

G   273

H   274

J   286

K   Not Here

STOP

Samples

Directions: Read each mathematics problem. Mark the answer you think is correct.

A Two towns are 54 miles apart. A bicyclist averaging 12 miles an hour leaves one town and rides for 3 hours. How can you find the remaining distance to the other town?

A $54 - (12 \times 3)$

B 12×3

C $54 + (12 \times 3)$

D $(54 - 12) \times 3$

E $(54 \div 3) - 12$

B Lori bought a Slurpster for $1.59 and paid with a 5-dollar bill. She asked for as many quarters as possible in her change. How many quarters did she receive?

F 16

G 15

H 14

J 13

K 12

If the answer you find is not one of the answer choices, work the problem again. Read the problem carefully, look for key words, numbers, and figures, and transfer numbers carefully to scratch paper.

Practice

1 The illustration below shows two sets of cubes. The white cubes are all the same weight, but this weight is unknown. The gray cubes each weigh 3 ounces. The groups of cubes shown below have the same total weight. What is the weight of a white cube?

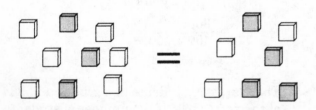

A 3.5 ounces

B 2 ounces

C 1 ounce

D 0.5 ounces

E 0.1 ounces

2 Country A is larger than country B. Country C is more than twice the size of countries A and B together. Which of these expresses this relationship among the countries?

F $C = 2(A + B)$

G $C > 2(A + B)$

H $C < A + B$

J $2C < A + B$

K $2C = A + B$

3 Anita worked 10 hours on Saturday. For 8 hours she earned $5.00 an hour, her regular rate. For 2 hours she earned 1.5 times her regular rate. How much did she earn working all day on Saturday?

A $41.50

B $43.00

C $50.50

D $51.50

E $55.00

GO

Lesson 30: Problem Solving

This graph shows students' scores on 5 different tests. The long vertical line shows the range of scores, the box shows the range in which two-thirds of the students' scores fall, and the horizontal bar shows the average (mean) score. Use this graph to answer questions 4 through 6.

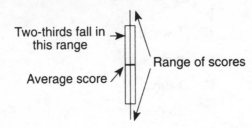

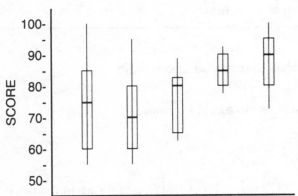

4 On which test did students' scores fall within the smallest range?

F   Test 1

G   Test 2

H   Test 3

J   Test 4

K   Test 5

5 What is the difference between the lowest and highest average scores?

A   30 points

B   20 points

C   15 points

D   10 points

E   5 points

6 What is the average score for all 5 tests?

F   75

G   80

H   82.5

J   85

K   87.5

7 In the figure below, one side is 6 units and the area is 90 units². Which answer choice shows how to find the perimeter of the figure?

6 units   A = 90 units²

A $(2 \times \frac{90}{6}) + (2 \times 6)$

B $(2 \times 6) + 90$

C $(2 \times 6) + (2 \times 90)$

D $2 \times (6 + \frac{6}{90})$

E $6 \times 6 \times \frac{90}{6} \times \frac{90}{6}$

8 The average weight of the 11 players who start for a football team is 185 pounds. The average weight of all the starting players except the quarterback is 188 pounds. Which sentence shows how to find Q, the weight of the quarterback?

F $Q = 10 \times 11 + (188 - 185)$

G $Q = (188 + 185) \div 2$

H $Q = (11 \times 185) - (10 \times 188)$

J $Q = (10 + 11) \times (188 - 185)$

K $Q = (188 - 11) - (185 \div 10)$

STOP

Lesson 31: Reasonable Answers

Samples

Directions: Read each mathematics problem. Mark the answer you think is correct.

A Which of these are you least likely to find in the real world?

    A   A car weighing 1000 kilograms

    B   A building 100 meters high

    C   A box with a surface area of 1 yard^2

    D   A refrigerator with 12 feet^3 of storage

    E   A basketball player 3 meters tall

B The distance from the earth to the **moon** is about 240,000 miles. A reasonable time for a round trip to the moon if you traveled at 9800 miles an hour is –

    F   1 week

    G   2 days

    H   1 day

    J   15 hours

    K   10 hours

Be sure to look at all the answer choices before you choose the one you think is correct.

Remember, the correct answer may not be an exact number.

Practice

1 The figure below shows a triangle and a circle. The perimeter of the circle is 314 cm, and the base of the triangle is equal to its height. A reasonable amount for the area of the triangle is —

    A   10,000 cm²

    B   5000 cm²

    C   1500 cm²

    D   1000 cm²

    E   500 cm²

2 Clarence has $100 in a bank account. Each year he puts $100 more in the account. The account earns 5% interest each year. What is a reasonable estimate of how much will he have in the account in 5 years?

    F   About $400

    G   Between $400 and $500

    H   Between $500 and $550

    J   About $600

    K   About $800

3 It takes a truck driver and a helper 8 hours to unload a truck. They receive $240 for their work. The driver receives 25% more than the helper. About how much does the driver make an hour?

    A   More than $18

    B   Between $16 and $17

    C   About $15

    D   Between $13 and $15

    E   About $10

GO

Lesson 31: Reasonable Answers

4 An acre is 43,500 square feet. A football field is 100 yards long and 160 feet wide. About how many acres is a football field?

F Less than 0.4 acres

G Exactly 0.5 acres

H About 1.1 acres

J About 2.2 acres

K More than 3 acres

5 The owner of a store buys computers for $895 and sells them for $1195. Her expenses each day are $450, and the store is open 6 days a week. What is a reasonable number of computers for her to sell in a week to pay her expenses?

A 18

B 15

C 14

D 11

E 9

6 The chart below shows the salary earned by 5 sales people. Their salary is based on years of service and total sales. A reasonable salary for a person with 7 years of service whose total sales are $478,391 is —

Name	Salary	Total Sales	Years of Service
Miller	$57,000	$448,573	12
Harkins	$35,000	$321,029	3
Adams	$43,000	$329,338	10
Sligo	$48,000	$401,945	8

F more than $60,000

G about $55,000

H between $50,000 and $54,000

J about $45,000

K less than $40,000

7 The area of the figure below is 648 units^2. Side A is twice side B. A reasonable length for side A is —

Area = 648 units^2 B

A

A between 35 and 40 units

B about 32 units

C exactly 24 units

D about 18 units

E between 10 and 15 units

8 Ralph earned a 65 on his first math test. He began studying harder and improved his score by 5 points on the next test. He took 4 more math tests, and on each one, he raised his score 5 points over his previous test. What is a reasonable average score for Ralph on the 6 math tests he took?

F More than 90

G Between 85 and 90

H Between 80 and 85

J Between 75 and 80

K Less than 75

9 About how many 6 inch by 6 inch by 6 inch boxes can be put in a carton that has 12 cubic feet of space and is 3 feet long and 2 feet wide?

A More than 100

B Exactly 96

C Exactly 72

D Exactly 48

E Less than 40

STOP

Sample A

What percentage of the larger circle shown on the right is shaded?

A $10\pi^2\%$

B $6\pi^2\%$

C   50%

D   45%

E   20%

---

1   A group of 10 friends is planning a ski vacation for 5 days. The round trip airfare will be $149 per person, and rooms will be $79 a night. Up to 4 people can sleep in a room. Ski rental will be $15 a day per person. Lift tickets will be $32 a day per person. About how much will it cost the group for airfare, rooms, skis, and lift tickets?

A   Less than $3000

B   Between $3000 and $3500

C   Between $3500 and $4000

D   Between $4000 and $4500

E   More than $4500

2   Last year, a business paid a dividend of $2.75 for each share of stock held by the owners. This year, the business expects to increase its dividend by 15%. Suppose you had 100 shares of stock in the company. How could you calculate the total amount of your dividend check?

F   ($2.75 x 0.15) x 100

G   ($2.75 x 1.15) x 100

H   ($2.75 + 1.15) x 100

J   ($2.75 + 100) x 0.15

K   ($2.75 + 0.15) x 100

3   What is the probability of getting either a 1 or a 2 by taking one turn at this spinner?

A $\frac{1}{2}$

B $\frac{3}{8}$

C $\frac{5}{16}$

D $\frac{4}{5}$

E   Not Here

4   How would you find the height in cm of a person who is 6 feet tall? A cm is 0.3937 of an inch.

F   (6 x 12) ÷ 0.3937

G   (6 x 12) x 0.3937

H   (0.3937 x 12) x 6

J   (1 + 0.3937) x 12 x 6

K   Not Here

GO

Lesson 32: Test Yourself

This graph shows the temperature from 8:00 in the morning to 5:00 in the afternoon. Use the graph to answer questions 5 - 7.

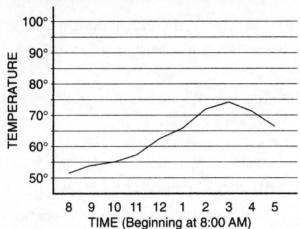

5 The temperature range for the day was —

A 14°

B 16°

C 18°

D 20°

E 22°

6 A reasonable approximation of the average temperature from 8:00 to noon is —

F less than 50°

G about 55°

H about 60°

J about 62°

K more than 62°

7 If the temperature trend continues, what will the temperature be at 7:00 PM?

A More than 65°

B Between 60° and 65°

C Between 55° and 60°

D Between 50° and 55°

E Less than 50°

8 The school year is about 180 days long. Students miss an average of 3.5 days of school a year because of illness. About how many total days will 20 students per grade miss in grades 8, 9, and 10?

F 210

G 200

H 73.5

J 70.5

K 63.5

9 Bill is 47 pounds heavier than Nick. Nick is more than 20 percent heavier than Denise. Which of these shows this relationship correctly?

A $B = (N + 47) > (1.20 \times D)$

B $B = (N + 47) > (0.20 \times D)$

C $(B - 47) = N > (1.20 \times D)$

D $(B + 47) = N < (1.20 \times D)$

E $(B + 47) = N < (1.20 \times D)$

10 There are 25 students in a class. The teacher writes each student's name on a slip of paper and puts it in a jar. At the beginning of school each day, the teacher pulls one name out of the jar and does not put it back. This student helps clean up at the end of the day. After 8 days, your name still has not been picked. What are the odds your name will be picked on day 9?

F $\frac{1}{8}$

G $\frac{1}{9}$

H $\frac{1}{17}$

J $\frac{1}{25}$

K Not Here

STOP

What Are Standardized Achievement Tests?

Achievement tests measure what children know in particular subject areas such as reading, language arts, and mathematics. They do not measure your child's intelligence or ability to learn.

When tests are standardized, or *normed*, children's test results are compared with those of a specific group who have taken the test, usually at the same age or grade.

Standardized achievement tests measure what children around the country are learning. The test makers survey popular textbook series, as well as state curriculum frameworks and other professional sources, to determine what content is covered widely.

Because of variations in state frameworks and textbook series, as well as grade ranges on some test levels, the tests may cover some material that children have not yet learned. This is especially true if the test is offered early in the school year. However, test scores are compared to those of other children who take the test at the same time of year, so your child will not be at a disadvantage if his or her class has not covered specific material yet.

Different School Districts, Different Tests

There are many flexible options for districts when offering standardized tests. Many school districts choose not to give the full test battery, but select certain content and scoring options. For example, many schools may test only in the areas of reading and mathematics. Similarly, a state or district may use one test for certain grades and another test for other grades. These decisions are often based on

the amount of time and money a district wishes to spend on test administration. Some states choose to develop their own statewide assessment tests.

On pages 75–77 you will find information about these five widely used standardized achievement tests:

- *California Achievement Tests (CAT)*
- *Terra Nova/CTBS*
- *Iowa Test of Basic Skills (ITBS)*
- *Stanford Achievement Test (SAT9)*
- *Metropolitan Achievement Test (MAT)*

However, this book contains strategies and practice questions for use with a variety of tests. Even if your state does not give one of the five tests listed above, your child will benefit from doing the practice questions in this book. If you're unsure about which test your child takes, contact your local school district to find out which tests are given.

Types of Test Questions

Traditionally, standardized achievement tests have used only multiple choice questions. Today, many tests may include constructed response (short answer) and extended response (essay) questions as well.

In addition, many tests include questions that tap students' higher-order thinking skills. Instead of simple recall questions, such as identifying a date in history, questions may require students to make comparisons and contrast or analyze results, among other skills.

What the Tests Measure

These tests do not measure your child's level of intelligence, but they do show how well your child knows material that he or she has learned and that is also covered on the tests. It's important to remember that some tests cover content that is not taught in your child's school or grade. In other instances, depending on when in the year the test is given, your child may not yet have covered the material.

If the test reports you receive show that your child needs improvement in one or more skill areas, you may want to seek help from your child's teacher and find out how you can work with your child to improve his or her skills.

California Achievement Test (CAT/5)

What Is the *California Achievement Test*?

The *California Achievement Test* is a standardized achievement test battery that is widely used with elementary through high school students.

Parts of the Test

The *CAT* includes tests in the following content areas:

Reading
- Word Analysis
- Vocabulary
- Comprehension

Spelling

Language Arts
- Language Mechanics
- Language Usage

Mathematics

Science

Social Studies

Your child may take some or all of these subtests if your district uses the *California Achievement Test*.

Terra Nova/CTBS (Comprehensive Tests of Basic Skills)

What Is the *Terra Nova/CTBS*?

The *Terra Nova/Comprehensive Tests of Basic Skills* is a standardized achievement test battery used in elementary through high school grades.

While many of the test questions on the *Terra Nova* are in the traditional multiple choice form, your child may take parts of the *Terra Nova* that include some open-ended questions (constructed-response items).

Parts of the Test

Your child may take some or all of the following subtests if your district uses the *Terra Nova/CTBS*:

Reading/Language Arts
Mathematics
Science
Social Studies

Supplementary tests include:
- Word Analysis
- Vocabulary
- Language Mechanics
- Spelling
- Mathematics Computation

Critical thinking skills may also be tested.

Iowa Test of Basic Skills (ITBS)

What Is the *ITBS*?

The *Iowa Test of Basic Skills* is a standardized achievement test battery used in elementary through high school grades.

Parts of the Test

Your child may take some or all of these subtests if your district uses the *ITBS*, also known as the *Iowa*:

Reading
- Vocabulary
- Reading Comprehension

Language Arts
- Spelling
- Capitalization
- Punctuation
- Usage and Expression

Mathematics
- Concepts/Estimate
- Problems/Data Interpretation

Social Studies

Science

Sources of Information

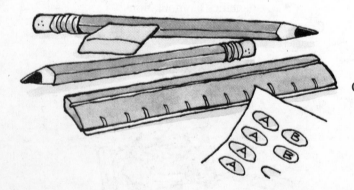

Stanford Achievement Test (SAT9)

What Is the *Stanford Achievement Test*?

The *Stanford Achievement Test, Ninth Edition (SAT9)* is a standardized achievement test battery used in elementary through high school grades.

Note that the *Stanford Achievement Test (SAT9)* is a different test from the *SAT* used by high school students for college admissions.

While many of the test questions on the *SAT9* are in traditional multiple choice form, your child may take parts of the *SAT9* that include some open-ended questions (constructed-response items).

Parts of the Test

Your child may take some or all of these subtests if your district uses the *Stanford Achievement Test*:

Reading
- Vocabulary
- Reading Comprehension

Mathematics
- Problem Solving
- Procedures

Language Arts

Spelling

Study Skills

Listening

Critical thinking skills may also be tested.